Ziggy's Secrets

*A book of secrets
for today's feline companion*

Rosemary Augustine

Ziggy's Secrets - *A book of secrets for today's feline companion*
Book Designer and Author - Rosemary Augustine

Published by Blue Spruce Publishing Company
2175 Golf Isle Drive, Suite 1024
Melbourne, FL 32935
610.647.8863
info@BlueSprucePublishing.com

Cover Photo: "Ziggy" by Rosemary Augustine
Back Cover Photo: Selfie of Ziggy and Rosemary Augustine
Cat Graphics: Provided by OpenClipArt.org

ISBN-13: 978-1-943581-00-9
ISBN-10: 1-943581-00-2

HOW TO USE THIS BOOK

Ziggy's Secrets is designed to look like a cat story book yet is disguised to be your personal internet password book for use at home or in the office. Because of the sensitivity of the contents once you begin to fill it, please keep it in a safe place. It is not recommended to use when traveling because of the sensitive data you will add to it. Because of the disguising nature of the cover, you can display it on your desk with comfort that others will not know of its contents. Please note, the author and/or publisher cannot be held responsible or liable for any loss, damage or consequence as a result of using this book, either by adding or storing your personal and sensitive information herein.

There is plenty of room with 150 pages, including space for entries such as the name of your account, the URL, your log in / user name, and password, as well as space for answers to security questions, a place for your account # and any additional notes. There is lots of white space in the margins for notes and the last 4 pages allows for additional notes, special instructions or a place to glue a 6" x 9" envelope full of licensing documentation or information.

We purposely did not add alphabetical letters to the margins since you have the option to enter your information alphabetically, numerically or by category so as not to restrict your use of this book. There is a lined space if you want to add any letter, word or number in the margin. If you decide to use this book alphabetically, you may first want to assess your URL need for letters like 'i', 'q', 'u', 'v', 'x', 'y' and 'z'. You may want to allow for 1 or 2 pages for the above mentioned letters and 3 pages for the remaining letters of the alphabet so that you can comfortably use the space allotted for URL / password entries. You decide, however, since the websites visited will vary with everyone using this password book.

Always use different logins / user names and passwords for each website visited. Encrypt your passwords with words or phrases and mix your passwords with numbers and symbols as login instructions will vary with each website visited. Change your passwords frequently. You may consider using pencil so that when changing your password you can easily remove the old information. Or, when using pen/ink, date when you added a new password so you know which one is current.

Use in good health and know that Ziggy will keep your secrets safe inside. "Like" Ziggy on Facebook at: **Ziggy's Secrets** or directly at www.Facebook.com/MyCoolCatZiggy. You can also visit Ziggy at his own website: **www.ThankGodImaFeline.com.**

. . .

Name:_____
URL:_____
Login:_____
P/W:_____
Pin:_____
Security Questions:_____
_____
Account #:_____
Notes:_____
_____

Name:_____
URL:_____
Login:_____
P/W:_____
Pin:_____
Security Questions:_____
_____
Account #:_____
Notes:_____
_____

Name:_____
URL:_____
Login:_____
P/W:_____
Pin:_____
Security Questions:_____
_____
Account #:_____
Notes:_____
_____

Name:_____
URL:_____
Login:_____
P/W:_____
Pin:_____
Security Questions:_____
_____
Account #:_____
Notes:_____
_____

Name:_____
URL:_____
Login:_____
P/W:_____
Pin:_____
Security Questions:_____
_____
Account #:_____
Notes:_____
_____

Name:_____
URL:_____
Login:_____
P/W:_____
Pin:_____
Security Questions:_____
_____
Account #:_____
Notes:_____
_____

Name:_____
URL:_____
Login:_____
P/W:_____
Pin:_____
Security Questions:_____
_____
Account #:_____
Notes:_____
_____

Name:_____
URL:_____
Login:_____
P/W:_____
Pin:_____
Security Questions:_____
_____
Account #:_____
Notes:_____
_____

Name:____
URL:____
Login:____
P/W:____
Pin:____
Security Questions:______________________________

Account #:____________________________________
Notes:____

Name:____
URL:____
Login:____
P/W:____
Pin:____
Security Questions:______________________________

Account #:____________________________________
Notes:____

Name:____
URL:____
Login:____
P/W:____
Pin:____
Security Questions:______________________________

Account #:____________________________________
Notes:____

Name:____
URL:____
Login:____
P/W:____
Pin:____
Security Questions:______________________________

Account #:____________________________________
Notes:____

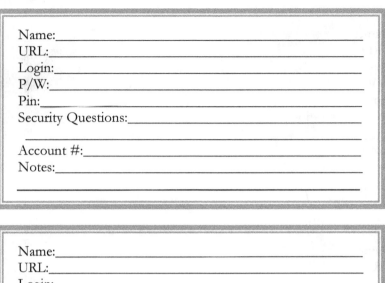

Name:_____
URL:_____
Login:_____
P/W:_____
Pin:_____
Security Questions:_____
_____
Account #:_____
Notes:_____
_____

Name:_____
URL:_____
Login:_____
P/W:_____
Pin:_____
Security Questions:_____
_____
Account #:_____
Notes:_____
_____

Name:_____
URL:_____
Login:_____
P/W:_____
Pin:_____
Security Questions:_____
_____
Account #:_____
Notes:_____
_____

Name:_____
URL:_____
Login:_____
P/W:_____
Pin:_____
Security Questions:_____
_____
Account #:_____
Notes:_____
_____

Ziggy's Secrets

Name:_____
URL:_____
Login:_____
P/W:_____
Pin:_____
Security Questions:_____
_____
Account #:_____
Notes:_____
_____

Name:_____
URL:_____
Login:_____
P/W:_____
Pin:_____
Security Questions:_____
_____
Account #:_____
Notes:_____
_____

Name:_____
URL:_____
Login:_____
P/W:_____
Pin:_____
Security Questions:_____
_____
Account #:_____
Notes:_____
_____

Name:_____
URL:_____
Login:_____
P/W:_____
Pin:_____
Security Questions:_____
_____
Account #:_____
Notes:_____
_____

Name:_____

URL:_____

Login:_____

P/W:_____

Pin:_____

Security Questions:_____

_____

Account #:_____

Notes:_____

_____

Name:_____

URL:_____

Login:_____

P/W:_____

Pin:_____

Security Questions:_____

_____

Account #:_____

Notes:_____

_____

Name:_____

URL:_____

Login:_____

P/W:_____

Pin:_____

Security Questions:_____

_____

Account #:_____

Notes:_____

_____

Name:_____

URL:_____

Login:_____

P/W:_____

Pin:_____

Security Questions:_____

_____

Account #:_____

Notes:_____

_____

Name:_____
URL:_____
Login:_____
P/W:_____
Pin:_____
Security Questions:_____
_____
Account #:_____
Notes:_____
_____

Name:_____
URL:_____
Login:_____
P/W:_____
Pin:_____
Security Questions:_____
_____
Account #:_____
Notes:_____
_____

Name:_____
URL:_____
Login:_____
P/W:_____
Pin:_____
Security Questions:_____
_____
Account #:_____
Notes:_____
_____

Name:_____
URL:_____
Login:_____
P/W:_____
Pin:_____
Security Questions:_____
_____
Account #:_____
Notes:_____
_____

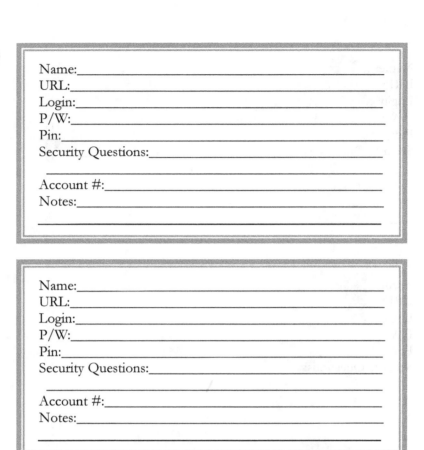

Name:_____
URL:_____
Login:_____
P/W:_____
Pin:_____
Security Questions:_____
_____
Account #:_____
Notes:_____
_____

Name:_____
URL:_____
Login:_____
P/W:_____
Pin:_____
Security Questions:_____
_____
Account #:_____
Notes:_____
_____

Name:_____
URL:_____
Login:_____
P/W:_____
Pin:_____
Security Questions:_____
_____
Account #:_____
Notes:_____
_____

Name:_____
URL:_____
Login:_____
P/W:_____
Pin:_____
Security Questions:_____
_____
Account #:_____
Notes:_____
_____

Name:_____
URL:_____
Login:_____
P/W:_____
Pin:_____
Security Questions:_____
_____
Account #:_____
Notes:_____
_____

Name:_____
URL:_____
Login:_____
P/W:_____
Pin:_____
Security Questions:_____
_____
Account #:_____
Notes:_____
_____

Name:_____
URL:_____
Login:_____
P/W:_____
Pin:_____
Security Questions:_____
_____
Account #:_____
Notes:_____
_____

Name:_____
URL:_____
Login:_____
P/W:_____
Pin:_____
Security Questions:_____
_____
Account #:_____
Notes:_____
_____

Name:_____

URL:_____

Login:_____

P/W:_____

Pin:_____

Security Questions:_____

_____

Account #:_____

Notes:_____

_____

Name:_____

URL:_____

Login:_____

P/W:_____

Pin:_____

Security Questions:_____

_____

Account #:_____

Notes:_____

_____

Name:_____

URL:_____

Login:_____

P/W:_____

Pin:_____

Security Questions:_____

_____

Account #:_____

Notes:_____

_____

Name:_____

URL:_____

Login:_____

P/W:_____

Pin:_____

Security Questions:_____

_____

Account #:_____

Notes:_____

_____

Name:_____

URL:_____

Login:_____

P/W:_____

Pin:_____

Security Questions:_____

_____

Account #:_____

Notes:_____

_____

Name:_____

URL:_____

Login:_____

P/W:_____

Pin:_____

Security Questions:_____

_____

Account #:_____

Notes:_____

_____

Name:_____

URL:_____

Login:_____

P/W:_____

Pin:_____

Security Questions:_____

_____

Account #:_____

Notes:_____

_____

Name:_____

URL:_____

Login:_____

P/W:_____

Pin:_____

Security Questions:_____

_____

Account #:_____

Notes:_____

_____

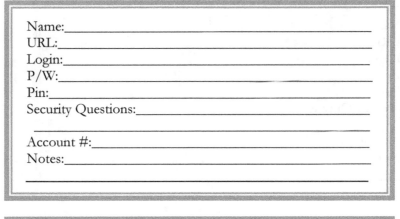

Name:_____
URL:_____
Login:_____
P/W:_____
Pin:_____
Security Questions:_____
_____
Account #:_____
Notes:_____
_____

Name:_____
URL:_____
Login:_____
P/W:_____
Pin:_____
Security Questions:_____
_____
Account #:_____
Notes:_____
_____

Name:_____
URL:_____
Login:_____
P/W:_____
Pin:_____
Security Questions:_____
_____
Account #:_____
Notes:_____
_____

Name:_____
URL:_____
Login:_____
P/W:_____
Pin:_____
Security Questions:_____
_____
Account #:_____
Notes:_____
_____

Name:_____
URL:_____
Login:_____
P/W:_____
Pin:_____
Security Questions:_____
_____
Account #:_____
Notes:_____
_____

Name:_____
URL:_____
Login:_____
P/W:_____
Pin:_____
Security Questions:_____
_____
Account #:_____
Notes:_____
_____

Name:_____
URL:_____
Login:_____
P/W:_____
Pin:_____
Security Questions:_____
_____
Account #:_____
Notes:_____
_____

Name:_____
URL:_____
Login:_____
P/W:_____
Pin:_____
Security Questions:_____
_____
Account #:_____
Notes:_____
_____

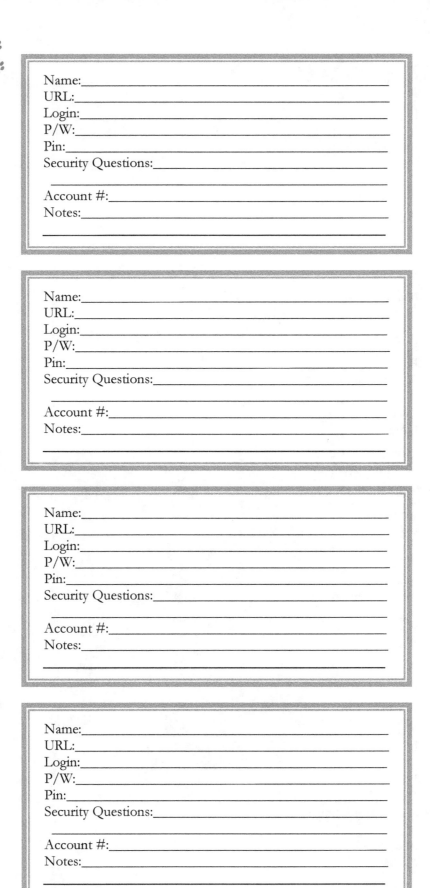

Name:_____

URL:_____

Login:_____

P/W:_____

Pin:_____

Security Questions:_____

_____

Account #:_____

Notes:_____

_____

Name:_____

URL:_____

Login:_____

P/W:_____

Pin:_____

Security Questions:_____

_____

Account #:_____

Notes:_____

_____

Name:_____

URL:_____

Login:_____

P/W:_____

Pin:_____

Security Questions:_____

_____

Account #:_____

Notes:_____

_____

Name:_____

URL:_____

Login:_____

P/W:_____

Pin:_____

Security Questions:_____

_____

Account #:_____

Notes:_____

_____

Name:_____

URL:_____

Login:_____

P/W:_____

Pin:_____

Security Questions:_____

_____

Account #:_____

Notes:_____

_____

Name:_____

URL:_____

Login:_____

P/W:_____

Pin:_____

Security Questions:_____

_____

Account #:_____

Notes:_____

_____

Name:_____

URL:_____

Login:_____

P/W:_____

Pin:_____

Security Questions:_____

_____

Account #:_____

Notes:_____

_____

Name:_____

URL:_____

Login:_____

P/W:_____

Pin:_____

Security Questions:_____

_____

Account #:_____

Notes:_____

_____

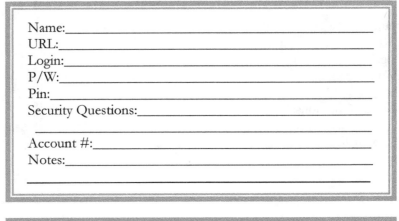

Name:_____
URL:_____
Login:_____
P/W:_____
Pin:_____
Security Questions:_____
_____
Account #:_____
Notes:_____
_____

Name:_____
URL:_____
Login:_____
P/W:_____
Pin:_____
Security Questions:_____
_____
Account #:_____
Notes:_____
_____

Name:_____
URL:_____
Login:_____
P/W:_____
Pin:_____
Security Questions:_____
_____
Account #:_____
Notes:_____
_____

Name:_____
URL:_____
Login:_____
P/W:_____
Pin:_____
Security Questions:_____
_____
Account #:_____
Notes:_____
_____

Name:_____
URL:_____
Login:_____
P/W:_____
Pin:_____
Security Questions:_____
_____
Account #:_____
Notes:_____
_____

Name:_____
URL:_____
Login:_____
P/W:_____
Pin:_____
Security Questions:_____
_____
Account #:_____
Notes:_____
_____

Name:_____
URL:_____
Login:_____
P/W:_____
Pin:_____
Security Questions:_____
_____
Account #:_____
Notes:_____
_____

Name:_____
URL:_____
Login:_____
P/W:_____
Pin:_____
Security Questions:_____
_____
Account #:_____
Notes:_____
_____

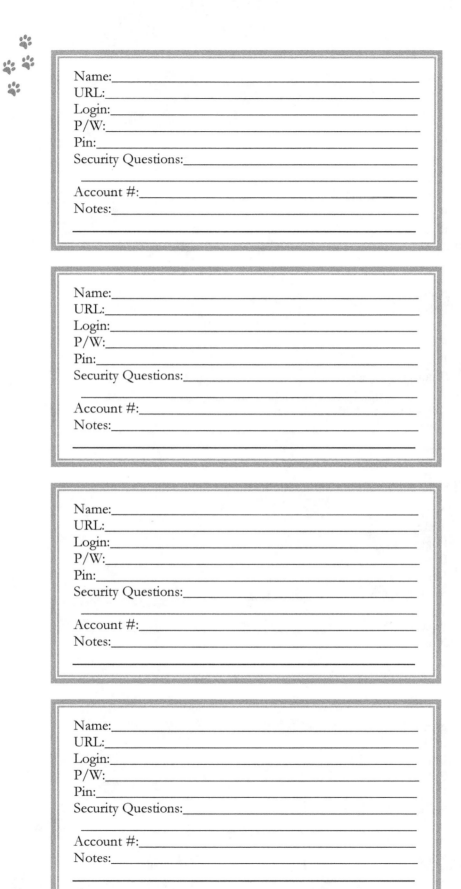

Name:_____

URL:_____

Login:_____

P/W:_____

Pin:_____

Security Questions:_____

_____

Account #:_____

Notes:_____

_____

Name:_____

URL:_____

Login:_____

P/W:_____

Pin:_____

Security Questions:_____

_____

Account #:_____

Notes:_____

_____

Name:_____

URL:_____

Login:_____

P/W:_____

Pin:_____

Security Questions:_____

_____

Account #:_____

Notes:_____

_____

Name:_____

URL:_____

Login:_____

P/W:_____

Pin:_____

Security Questions:_____

_____

Account #:_____

Notes:_____

_____

Name:_____

URL:_____

Login:_____

P/W:_____

Pin:_____

Security Questions:_____

_____

Account #:_____

Notes:_____

_____

Name:_____

URL:_____

Login:_____

P/W:_____

Pin:_____

Security Questions:_____

_____

Account #:_____

Notes:_____

_____

Name:_____

URL:_____

Login:_____

P/W:_____

Pin:_____

Security Questions:_____

_____

Account #:_____

Notes:_____

_____

Name:_____

URL:_____

Login:_____

P/W:_____

Pin:_____

Security Questions:_____

_____

Account #:_____

Notes:_____

_____

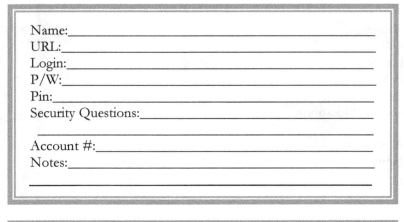

Name:_____
URL:_____
Login:_____
P/W:_____
Pin:_____
Security Questions:_____
_____
Account #:_____
Notes:_____
_____

Name:_____
URL:_____
Login:_____
P/W:_____
Pin:_____
Security Questions:_____
_____
Account #:_____
Notes:_____
_____

Name:_____
URL:_____
Login:_____
P/W:_____
Pin:_____
Security Questions:_____
_____
Account #:_____
Notes:_____
_____

Name:_____
URL:_____
Login:_____
P/W:_____
Pin:_____
Security Questions:_____
_____
Account #:_____
Notes:_____
_____

Name:_____
URL:_____
Login:_____
P/W:_____
Pin:_____
Security Questions:_____
_____
Account #:_____
Notes:_____
_____

Name:_____
URL:_____
Login:_____
P/W:_____
Pin:_____
Security Questions:_____
_____
Account #:_____
Notes:_____
_____

Name:_____
URL:_____
Login:_____
P/W:_____
Pin:_____
Security Questions:_____
_____
Account #:_____
Notes:_____
_____

Name:_____
URL:_____
Login:_____
P/W:_____
Pin:_____
Security Questions:_____
_____
Account #:_____
Notes:_____
_____

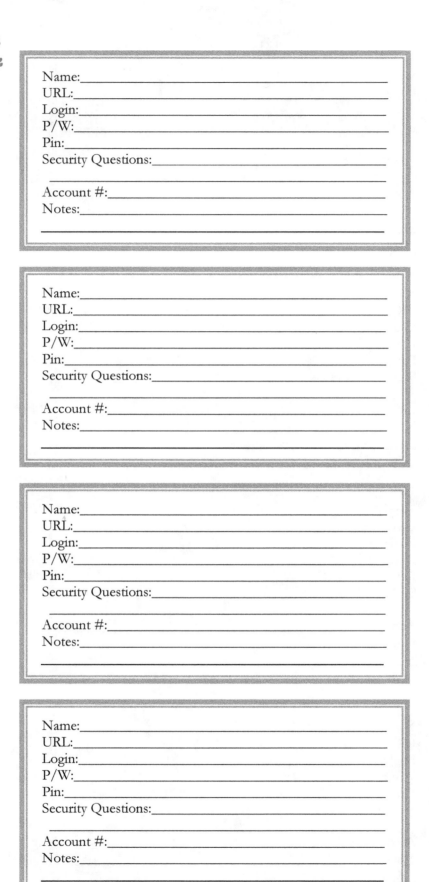

Name:_____

URL:_____

Login:_____

P/W:_____

Pin:_____

Security Questions:_____

_____

Account #:_____

Notes:_____

_____

Name:_____

URL:_____

Login:_____

P/W:_____

Pin:_____

Security Questions:_____

_____

Account #:_____

Notes:_____

_____

Name:_____

URL:_____

Login:_____

P/W:_____

Pin:_____

Security Questions:_____

_____

Account #:_____

Notes:_____

_____

Name:_____

URL:_____

Login:_____

P/W:_____

Pin:_____

Security Questions:_____

_____

Account #:_____

Notes:_____

_____

Name:_____
URL:_____
Login:_____
P/W:_____
Pin:_____
Security Questions:_____
_____
Account #:_____
Notes:_____
_____

Name:_____
URL:_____
Login:_____
P/W:_____
Pin:_____
Security Questions:_____
_____
Account #:_____
Notes:_____
_____

Name:_____
URL:_____
Login:_____
P/W:_____
Pin:_____
Security Questions:_____
_____
Account #:_____
Notes:_____
_____

Name:_____
URL:_____
Login:_____
P/W:_____
Pin:_____
Security Questions:_____
_____
Account #:_____
Notes:_____
_____

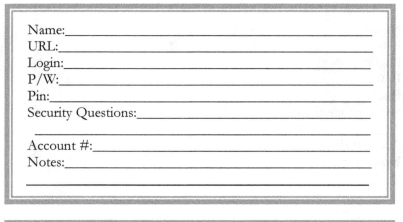

Name:_____
URL:_____
Login:_____
P/W:_____
Pin:_____
Security Questions:_____
_____
Account #:_____
Notes:_____
_____

Name:_____
URL:_____
Login:_____
P/W:_____
Pin:_____
Security Questions:_____
_____
Account #:_____
Notes:_____
_____

Name:_____
URL:_____
Login:_____
P/W:_____
Pin:_____
Security Questions:_____
_____
Account #:_____
Notes:_____
_____

Name:_____
URL:_____
Login:_____
P/W:_____
Pin:_____
Security Questions:_____
_____
Account #:_____
Notes:_____
_____

Name:_____
URL:_____
Login:_____
P/W:_____
Pin:_____
Security Questions:_____
_____
Account #:_____
Notes:_____
_____

Name:_____
URL:_____
Login:_____
P/W:_____
Pin:_____
Security Questions:_____
_____
Account #:_____
Notes:_____
_____

Name:_____
URL:_____
Login:_____
P/W:_____
Pin:_____
Security Questions:_____
_____
Account #:_____
Notes:_____
_____

Name:_____
URL:_____
Login:_____
P/W:_____
Pin:_____
Security Questions:_____
_____
Account #:_____
Notes:_____
_____

Name:_____
URL:_____
Login:_____
P/W:_____
Pin:_____
Security Questions:_____
_____
Account #:_____
Notes:_____
_____

Name:_____
URL:_____
Login:_____
P/W:_____
Pin:_____
Security Questions:_____
_____
Account #:_____
Notes:_____
_____

Name:_____
URL:_____
Login:_____
P/W:_____
Pin:_____
Security Questions:_____
_____
Account #:_____
Notes:_____
_____

Name:_____
URL:_____
Login:_____
P/W:_____
Pin:_____
Security Questions:_____
_____
Account #:_____
Notes:_____
_____

Name:_____
URL:_____
Login:_____
P/W:_____
Pin:_____
Security Questions:_____
_____
Account #:_____
Notes:_____
_____

Name:_____
URL:_____
Login:_____
P/W:_____
Pin:_____
Security Questions:_____
_____
Account #:_____
Notes:_____
_____

Name:_____
URL:_____
Login:_____
P/W:_____
Pin:_____
Security Questions:_____
_____
Account #:_____
Notes:_____
_____

Name:_____
URL:_____
Login:_____
P/W:_____
Pin:_____
Security Questions:_____
_____
Account #:_____
Notes:_____
_____

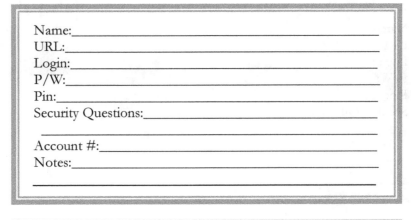

Name:_____
URL:_____
Login:_____
P/W:_____
Pin:_____
Security Questions:_____
_____
Account #:_____
Notes:_____
_____

Name:_____
URL:_____
Login:_____
P/W:_____
Pin:_____
Security Questions:_____
_____
Account #:_____
Notes:_____
_____

Name:_____
URL:_____
Login:_____
P/W:_____
Pin:_____
Security Questions:_____
_____
Account #:_____
Notes:_____
_____

Name:_____
URL:_____
Login:_____
P/W:_____
Pin:_____
Security Questions:_____
_____
Account #:_____
Notes:_____
_____

Name:_____

URL:_____

Login:_____

P/W:_____

Pin:_____

Security Questions:_____

_____

Account #:_____

Notes:_____

_____

Name:_____

URL:_____

Login:_____

P/W:_____

Pin:_____

Security Questions:_____

_____

Account #:_____

Notes:_____

_____

Name:_____

URL:_____

Login:_____

P/W:_____

Pin:_____

Security Questions:_____

_____

Account #:_____

Notes:_____

_____

Name:_____

URL:_____

Login:_____

P/W:_____

Pin:_____

Security Questions:_____

_____

Account #:_____

Notes:_____

_____

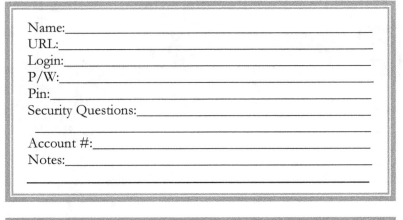

Name:_____
URL:_____
Login:_____
P/W:_____
Pin:_____
Security Questions:_____
_____
Account #:_____
Notes:_____
_____

Name:_____
URL:_____
Login:_____
P/W:_____
Pin:_____
Security Questions:_____
_____
Account #:_____
Notes:_____
_____

Name:_____
URL:_____
Login:_____
P/W:_____
Pin:_____
Security Questions:_____
_____
Account #:_____
Notes:_____
_____

Name:_____
URL:_____
Login:_____
P/W:_____
Pin:_____
Security Questions:_____
_____
Account #:_____
Notes:_____
_____

Name:_____
URL:_____
Login:_____
P/W:_____
Pin:_____
Security Questions:_____
_____
Account #:_____
Notes:_____
_____

Name:_____
URL:_____
Login:_____
P/W:_____
Pin:_____
Security Questions:_____
_____
Account #:_____
Notes:_____
_____

Name:_____
URL:_____
Login:_____
P/W:_____
Pin:_____
Security Questions:_____
_____
Account #:_____
Notes:_____
_____

Name:_____
URL:_____
Login:_____
P/W:_____
Pin:_____
Security Questions:_____
_____
Account #:_____
Notes:_____
_____

Name:_____

URL:_____

Login:_____

P/W:_____

Pin:_____

Security Questions:_____

_____

Account #:_____

Notes:_____

_____

Name:_____

URL:_____

Login:_____

P/W:_____

Pin:_____

Security Questions:_____

_____

Account #:_____

Notes:_____

_____

Name:_____

URL:_____

Login:_____

P/W:_____

Pin:_____

Security Questions:_____

_____

Account #:_____

Notes:_____

_____

Name:_____

URL:_____

Login:_____

P/W:_____

Pin:_____

Security Questions:_____

_____

Account #:_____

Notes:_____

_____

Name:_____
URL:_____
Login:_____
P/W:_____
Pin:_____
Security Questions:_____
_____
Account #:_____
Notes:_____
_____

Name:_____
URL:_____
Login:_____
P/W:_____
Pin:_____
Security Questions:_____
_____
Account #:_____
Notes:_____
_____

Name:_____
URL:_____
Login:_____
P/W:_____
Pin:_____
Security Questions:_____
_____
Account #:_____
Notes:_____
_____

Name:_____
URL:_____
Login:_____
P/W:_____
Pin:_____
Security Questions:_____
_____
Account #:_____
Notes:_____
_____

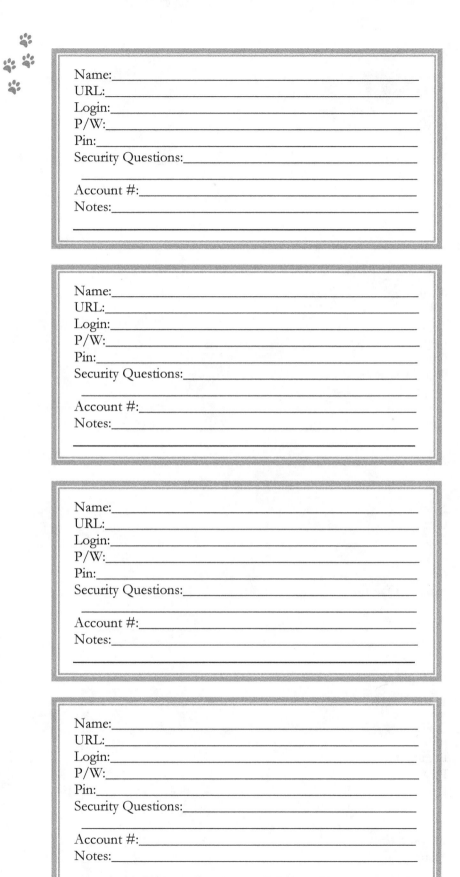

Name:_____
URL:_____
Login:_____
P/W:_____
Pin:_____
Security Questions:_____
_____
Account #:_____
Notes:_____
_____

Name:_____
URL:_____
Login:_____
P/W:_____
Pin:_____
Security Questions:_____
_____
Account #:_____
Notes:_____
_____

Name:_____
URL:_____
Login:_____
P/W:_____
Pin:_____
Security Questions:_____
_____
Account #:_____
Notes:_____
_____

Name:_____
URL:_____
Login:_____
P/W:_____
Pin:_____
Security Questions:_____
_____
Account #:_____
Notes:_____
_____

Name:_____
URL:_____
Login:_____
P/W:_____
Pin:_____
Security Questions:_____
_____
Account #:_____
Notes:_____
_____

Name:_____
URL:_____
Login:_____
P/W:_____
Pin:_____
Security Questions:_____
_____
Account #:_____
Notes:_____
_____

Name:_____
URL:_____
Login:_____
P/W:_____
Pin:_____
Security Questions:_____
_____
Account #:_____
Notes:_____
_____

Name:_____
URL:_____
Login:_____
P/W:_____
Pin:_____
Security Questions:_____
_____
Account #:_____
Notes:_____
_____

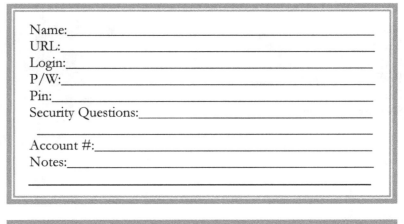

Name:_____

URL:_____

Login:_____

P/W:_____

Pin:_____

Security Questions:_____

_____

Account #:_____

Notes:_____

_____

Name:_____

URL:_____

Login:_____

P/W:_____

Pin:_____

Security Questions:_____

_____

Account #:_____

Notes:_____

_____

Name:_____

URL:_____

Login:_____

P/W:_____

Pin:_____

Security Questions:_____

_____

Account #:_____

Notes:_____

_____

Name:_____

URL:_____

Login:_____

P/W:_____

Pin:_____

Security Questions:_____

_____

Account #:_____

Notes:_____

_____

Ziggy's Secrets

Name:_____
URL:_____
Login:_____
P/W:_____
Pin:_____
Security Questions:_____
_____
Account #:_____
Notes:_____
_____

Name:_____
URL:_____
Login:_____
P/W:_____
Pin:_____
Security Questions:_____
_____
Account #:_____
Notes:_____
_____

Name:_____
URL:_____
Login:_____
P/W:_____
Pin:_____
Security Questions:_____
_____
Account #:_____
Notes:_____
_____

Name:_____
URL:_____
Login:_____
P/W:_____
Pin:_____
Security Questions:_____
_____
Account #:_____
Notes:_____
_____

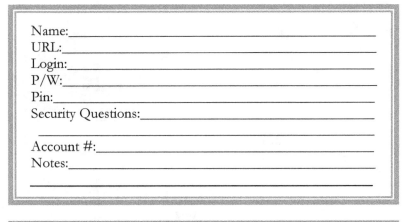

Name:_____
URL:_____
Login:_____
P/W:_____
Pin:_____
Security Questions:_____
_____
Account #:_____
Notes:_____
_____

Name:_____
URL:_____
Login:_____
P/W:_____
Pin:_____
Security Questions:_____
_____
Account #:_____
Notes:_____
_____

Name:_____
URL:_____
Login:_____
P/W:_____
Pin:_____
Security Questions:_____
_____
Account #:_____
Notes:_____
_____

Name:_____
URL:_____
Login:_____
P/W:_____
Pin:_____
Security Questions:_____
_____
Account #:_____
Notes:_____
_____

Ziggy's Secrets

Name:_____
URL:_____
Login:_____
P/W:_____
Pin:_____
Security Questions:_____
_____
Account #:_____
Notes:_____
_____

Name:_____
URL:_____
Login:_____
P/W:_____
Pin:_____
Security Questions:_____
_____
Account #:_____
Notes:_____
_____

Name:_____
URL:_____
Login:_____
P/W:_____
Pin:_____
Security Questions:_____
_____
Account #:_____
Notes:_____
_____

Name:_____
URL:_____
Login:_____
P/W:_____
Pin:_____
Security Questions:_____
_____
Account #:_____
Notes:_____
_____

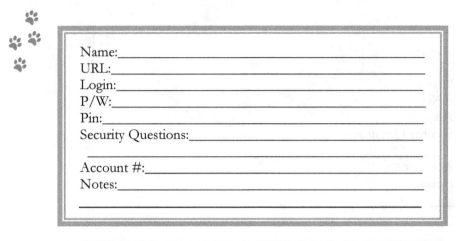

Name:_____
URL:_____
Login:_____
P/W:_____
Pin:_____
Security Questions:_____
_____
Account #:_____
Notes:_____
_____

Name:_____
URL:_____
Login:_____
P/W:_____
Pin:_____
Security Questions:_____
_____
Account #:_____
Notes:_____
_____

Name:_____
URL:_____
Login:_____
P/W:_____
Pin:_____
Security Questions:_____
_____
Account #:_____
Notes:_____
_____

Name:_____
URL:_____
Login:_____
P/W:_____
Pin:_____
Security Questions:_____
_____
Account #:_____
Notes:_____
_____

Name:_____
URL:_____
Login:_____
P/W:_____
Pin:_____
Security Questions:_____
_____
Account #:_____
Notes:_____
_____

Name:_____
URL:_____
Login:_____
P/W:_____
Pin:_____
Security Questions:_____
_____
Account #:_____
Notes:_____
_____

Name:_____
URL:_____
Login:_____
P/W:_____
Pin:_____
Security Questions:_____
_____
Account #:_____
Notes:_____
_____

Name:_____
URL:_____
Login:_____
P/W:_____
Pin:_____
Security Questions:_____
_____
Account #:_____
Notes:_____
_____

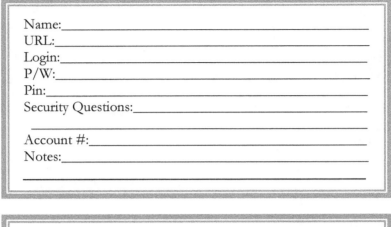

Name:_____

URL:_____

Login:_____

P/W:_____

Pin:_____

Security Questions:_____

_____

Account #:_____

Notes:_____

_____

Name:_____

URL:_____

Login:_____

P/W:_____

Pin:_____

Security Questions:_____

_____

Account #:_____

Notes:_____

_____

Name:_____

URL:_____

Login:_____

P/W:_____

Pin:_____

Security Questions:_____

_____

Account #:_____

Notes:_____

_____

Name:_____

URL:_____

Login:_____

P/W:_____

Pin:_____

Security Questions:_____

_____

Account #:_____

Notes:_____

_____

Name:_____
URL:_____
Login:_____
P/W:_____
Pin:_____
Security Questions:_____
_____
Account #:_____
Notes:_____
_____

Name:_____
URL:_____
Login:_____
P/W:_____
Pin:_____
Security Questions:_____
_____
Account #:_____
Notes:_____
_____

Name:_____
URL:_____
Login:_____
P/W:_____
Pin:_____
Security Questions:_____
_____
Account #:_____
Notes:_____
_____

Name:_____
URL:_____
Login:_____
P/W:_____
Pin:_____
Security Questions:_____
_____
Account #:_____
Notes:_____
_____

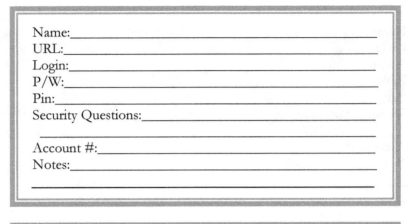

Name:_____

URL:_____

Login:_____

P/W:_____

Pin:_____

Security Questions:_____

_____

Account #:_____

Notes:_____

_____

Name:_____

URL:_____

Login:_____

P/W:_____

Pin:_____

Security Questions:_____

_____

Account #:_____

Notes:_____

_____

Name:_____

URL:_____

Login:_____

P/W:_____

Pin:_____

Security Questions:_____

_____

Account #:_____

Notes:_____

_____

Name:_____

URL:_____

Login:_____

P/W:_____

Pin:_____

Security Questions:_____

_____

Account #:_____

Notes:_____

_____

Ziggy's Secrets

Name:_____
URL:_____
Login:_____
P/W:_____
Pin:_____
Security Questions:_____
_____
Account #:_____
Notes:_____
_____

Name:_____
URL:_____
Login:_____
P/W:_____
Pin:_____
Security Questions:_____
_____
Account #:_____
Notes:_____
_____

Name:_____
URL:_____
Login:_____
P/W:_____
Pin:_____
Security Questions:_____
_____
Account #:_____
Notes:_____
_____

Name:_____
URL:_____
Login:_____
P/W:_____
Pin:_____
Security Questions:_____
_____
Account #:_____
Notes:_____
_____

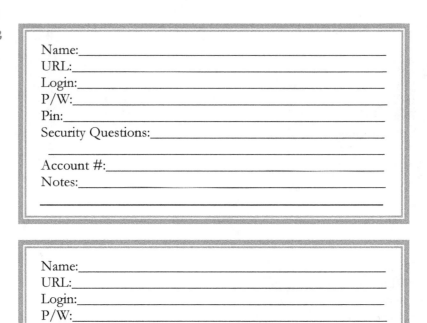

Name:_____
URL:_____
Login:_____
P/W:_____
Pin:_____
Security Questions:_____
_____
Account #:_____
Notes:_____
_____

Name:_____
URL:_____
Login:_____
P/W:_____
Pin:_____
Security Questions:_____
_____
Account #:_____
Notes:_____
_____

Name:_____
URL:_____
Login:_____
P/W:_____
Pin:_____
Security Questions:_____
_____
Account #:_____
Notes:_____
_____

Name:_____
URL:_____
Login:_____
P/W:_____
Pin:_____
Security Questions:_____
_____
Account #:_____
Notes:_____
_____

Name:_____
URL:_____
Login:_____
P/W:_____
Pin:_____
Security Questions:_____
_____
Account #:_____
Notes:_____
_____

Name:_____
URL:_____
Login:_____
P/W:_____
Pin:_____
Security Questions:_____
_____
Account #:_____
Notes:_____
_____

Name:_____
URL:_____
Login:_____
P/W:_____
Pin:_____
Security Questions:_____
_____
Account #:_____
Notes:_____
_____

Name:_____
URL:_____
Login:_____
P/W:_____
Pin:_____
Security Questions:_____
_____
Account #:_____
Notes:_____
_____

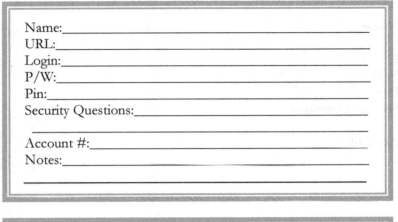

Name:_____
URL:_____
Login:_____
P/W:_____
Pin:_____
Security Questions:_____
_____
Account #:_____
Notes:_____
_____

Name:_____
URL:_____
Login:_____
P/W:_____
Pin:_____
Security Questions:_____
_____
Account #:_____
Notes:_____
_____

Name:_____
URL:_____
Login:_____
P/W:_____
Pin:_____
Security Questions:_____
_____
Account #:_____
Notes:_____
_____

Name:_____
URL:_____
Login:_____
P/W:_____
Pin:_____
Security Questions:_____
_____
Account #:_____
Notes:_____
_____

Name:_____
URL:_____
Login:_____
P/W:_____
Pin:_____
Security Questions:_____
_____
Account #:_____
Notes:_____
_____

Name:_____
URL:_____
Login:_____
P/W:_____
Pin:_____
Security Questions:_____
_____
Account #:_____
Notes:_____
_____

Name:_____
URL:_____
Login:_____
P/W:_____
Pin:_____
Security Questions:_____
_____
Account #:_____
Notes:_____
_____

Name:_____
URL:_____
Login:_____
P/W:_____
Pin:_____
Security Questions:_____
_____
Account #:_____
Notes:_____
_____

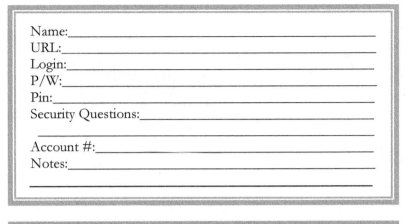

Name:_____
URL:_____
Login:_____
P/W:_____
Pin:_____
Security Questions:_____
_____
Account #:_____
Notes:_____
_____

Name:_____
URL:_____
Login:_____
P/W:_____
Pin:_____
Security Questions:_____
_____
Account #:_____
Notes:_____
_____

Name:_____
URL:_____
Login:_____
P/W:_____
Pin:_____
Security Questions:_____
_____
Account #:_____
Notes:_____
_____

Name:_____
URL:_____
Login:_____
P/W:_____
Pin:_____
Security Questions:_____
_____
Account #:_____
Notes:_____
_____

Name:_____
URL:_____
Login:_____
P/W:_____
Pin:_____
Security Questions:_____
_____
Account #:_____
Notes:_____
_____

Name:_____
URL:_____
Login:_____
P/W:_____
Pin:_____
Security Questions:_____
_____
Account #:_____
Notes:_____
_____

Name:_____
URL:_____
Login:_____
P/W:_____
Pin:_____
Security Questions:_____
_____
Account #:_____
Notes:_____
_____

Name:_____
URL:_____
Login:_____
P/W:_____
Pin:_____
Security Questions:_____
_____
Account #:_____
Notes:_____
_____

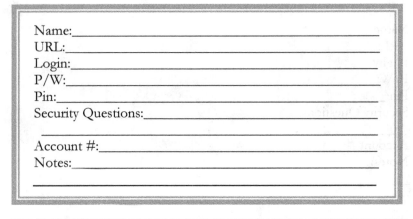

Name:_____
URL:_____
Login:_____
P/W:_____
Pin:_____
Security Questions:_____
_____
Account #:_____
Notes:_____
_____

Name:_____
URL:_____
Login:_____
P/W:_____
Pin:_____
Security Questions:_____
_____
Account #:_____
Notes:_____
_____

Name:_____
URL:_____
Login:_____
P/W:_____
Pin:_____
Security Questions:_____
_____
Account #:_____
Notes:_____
_____

Name:_____
URL:_____
Login:_____
P/W:_____
Pin:_____
Security Questions:_____
_____
Account #:_____
Notes:_____
_____

Name:_____
URL:_____
Login:_____
P/W:_____
Pin:_____
Security Questions:_____
_____
Account #:_____
Notes:_____
_____

Name:_____
URL:_____
Login:_____
P/W:_____
Pin:_____
Security Questions:_____
_____
Account #:_____
Notes:_____
_____

Name:_____
URL:_____
Login:_____
P/W:_____
Pin:_____
Security Questions:_____
_____
Account #:_____
Notes:_____
_____

Name:_____
URL:_____
Login:_____
P/W:_____
Pin:_____
Security Questions:_____
_____
Account #:_____
Notes:_____
_____

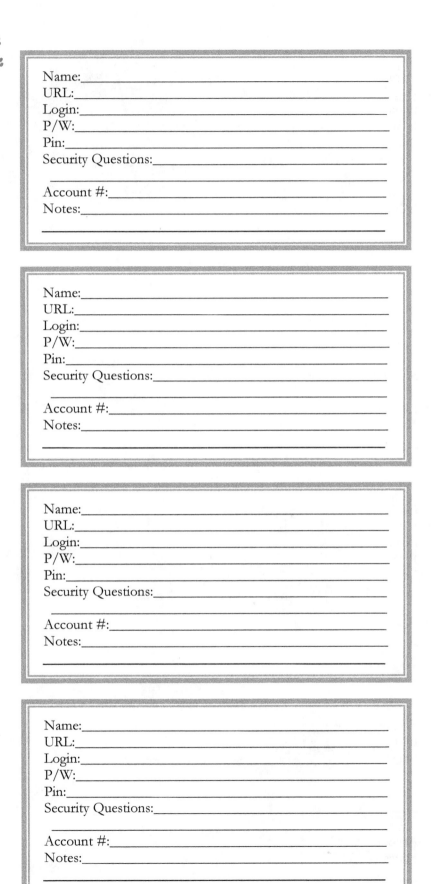

Name:_____
URL:_____
Login:_____
P/W:_____
Pin:_____
Security Questions:_____
_____
Account #:_____
Notes:_____
_____

Name:_____
URL:_____
Login:_____
P/W:_____
Pin:_____
Security Questions:_____
_____
Account #:_____
Notes:_____
_____

Name:_____
URL:_____
Login:_____
P/W:_____
Pin:_____
Security Questions:_____
_____
Account #:_____
Notes:_____
_____

Name:_____
URL:_____
Login:_____
P/W:_____
Pin:_____
Security Questions:_____
_____
Account #:_____
Notes:_____
_____

Name:_____
URL:_____
Login:_____
P/W:_____
Pin:_____
Security Questions:_____
_____
Account #:_____
Notes:_____
_____

Name:_____
URL:_____
Login:_____
P/W:_____
Pin:_____
Security Questions:_____
_____
Account #:_____
Notes:_____
_____

Name:_____
URL:_____
Login:_____
P/W:_____
Pin:_____
Security Questions:_____
_____
Account #:_____
Notes:_____
_____

Name:_____
URL:_____
Login:_____
P/W:_____
Pin:_____
Security Questions:_____
_____
Account #:_____
Notes:_____
_____

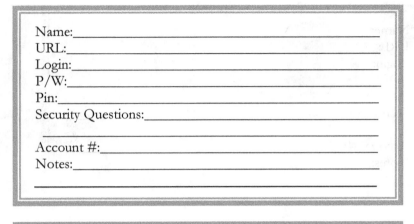

Name:_____
URL:_____
Login:_____
P/W:_____
Pin:_____
Security Questions:_____
_____
Account #:_____
Notes:_____
_____

Name:_____
URL:_____
Login:_____
P/W:_____
Pin:_____
Security Questions:_____
_____
Account #:_____
Notes:_____
_____

Name:_____
URL:_____
Login:_____
P/W:_____
Pin:_____
Security Questions:_____
_____
Account #:_____
Notes:_____
_____

Name:_____
URL:_____
Login:_____
P/W:_____
Pin:_____
Security Questions:_____
_____
Account #:_____
Notes:_____
_____

Name:_____
URL:_____
Login:_____
P/W:_____
Pin:_____
Security Questions:_____
_____
Account #:_____
Notes:_____
_____

Name:_____
URL:_____
Login:_____
P/W:_____
Pin:_____
Security Questions:_____
_____
Account #:_____
Notes:_____
_____

Name:_____
URL:_____
Login:_____
P/W:_____
Pin:_____
Security Questions:_____
_____
Account #:_____
Notes:_____
_____

Name:_____
URL:_____
Login:_____
P/W:_____
Pin:_____
Security Questions:_____
_____
Account #:_____
Notes:_____
_____

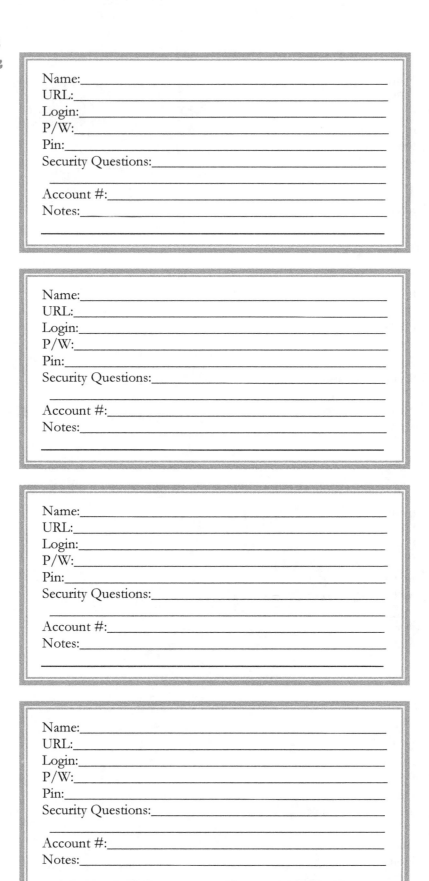

Name:_____

URL:_____

Login:_____

P/W:_____

Pin:_____

Security Questions:_____

_____

Account #:_____

Notes:_____

_____

Name:_____

URL:_____

Login:_____

P/W:_____

Pin:_____

Security Questions:_____

_____

Account #:_____

Notes:_____

_____

Name:_____

URL:_____

Login:_____

P/W:_____

Pin:_____

Security Questions:_____

_____

Account #:_____

Notes:_____

_____

Name:_____

URL:_____

Login:_____

P/W:_____

Pin:_____

Security Questions:_____

_____

Account #:_____

Notes:_____

_____

Name:_____
URL:_____
Login:_____
P/W:_____
Pin:_____
Security Questions:_____
_____
Account #:_____
Notes:_____
_____

Name:_____
URL:_____
Login:_____
P/W:_____
Pin:_____
Security Questions:_____
_____
Account #:_____
Notes:_____
_____

Name:_____
URL:_____
Login:_____
P/W:_____
Pin:_____
Security Questions:_____
_____
Account #:_____
Notes:_____
_____

Name:_____
URL:_____
Login:_____
P/W:_____
Pin:_____
Security Questions:_____
_____
Account #:_____
Notes:_____
_____

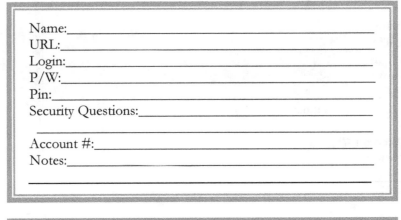

Name:_____
URL:_____
Login:_____
P/W:_____
Pin:_____
Security Questions:_____
_____
Account #:_____
Notes:_____
_____

Name:_____
URL:_____
Login:_____
P/W:_____
Pin:_____
Security Questions:_____
_____
Account #:_____
Notes:_____
_____

Name:_____
URL:_____
Login:_____
P/W:_____
Pin:_____
Security Questions:_____
_____
Account #:_____
Notes:_____
_____

Name:_____
URL:_____
Login:_____
P/W:_____
Pin:_____
Security Questions:_____
_____
Account #:_____
Notes:_____
_____

Name:_____
URL:_____
Login:_____
P/W:_____
Pin:_____
Security Questions:_____
_____
Account #:_____
Notes:_____
_____

Name:_____
URL:_____
Login:_____
P/W:_____
Pin:_____
Security Questions:_____
_____
Account #:_____
Notes:_____
_____

Name:_____
URL:_____
Login:_____
P/W:_____
Pin:_____
Security Questions:_____
_____
Account #:_____
Notes:_____
_____

Name:_____
URL:_____
Login:_____
P/W:_____
Pin:_____
Security Questions:_____
_____
Account #:_____
Notes:_____
_____

Name:_____
URL:_____
Login:_____
P/W:_____
Pin:_____
Security Questions:_____
_____
Account #:_____
Notes:_____
_____

Name:_____
URL:_____
Login:_____
P/W:_____
Pin:_____
Security Questions:_____
_____
Account #:_____
Notes:_____
_____

Name:_____
URL:_____
Login:_____
P/W:_____
Pin:_____
Security Questions:_____
_____
Account #:_____
Notes:_____
_____

Name:_____
URL:_____
Login:_____
P/W:_____
Pin:_____
Security Questions:_____
_____
Account #:_____
Notes:_____
_____

Name:_____
URL:_____
Login:_____
P/W:_____
Pin:_____
Security Questions:_____
_____
Account #:_____
Notes:_____
_____

Name:_____
URL:_____
Login:_____
P/W:_____
Pin:_____
Security Questions:_____
_____
Account #:_____
Notes:_____
_____

Name:_____
URL:_____
Login:_____
P/W:_____
Pin:_____
Security Questions:_____
_____
Account #:_____
Notes:_____
_____

Name:_____
URL:_____
Login:_____
P/W:_____
Pin:_____
Security Questions:_____
_____
Account #:_____
Notes:_____
_____

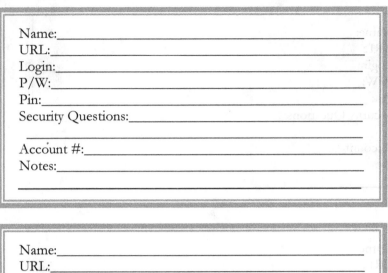

Name:_____
URL:_____
Login:_____
P/W:_____
Pin:_____
Security Questions:_____
_____
Account #:_____
Notes:_____
_____

Name:_____
URL:_____
Login:_____
P/W:_____
Pin:_____
Security Questions:_____
_____
Account #:_____
Notes:_____
_____

Name:_____
URL:_____
Login:_____
P/W:_____
Pin:_____
Security Questions:_____
_____
Account #:_____
Notes:_____
_____

Name:_____
URL:_____
Login:_____
P/W:_____
Pin:_____
Security Questions:_____
_____
Account #:_____
Notes:_____
_____

Name:_____
URL:_____
Login:_____
P/W:_____
Pin:_____
Security Questions:_____
_____
Account #:_____
Notes:_____
_____

Name:_____
URL:_____
Login:_____
P/W:_____
Pin:_____
Security Questions:_____
_____
Account #:_____
Notes:_____
_____

Name:_____
URL:_____
Login:_____
P/W:_____
Pin:_____
Security Questions:_____
_____
Account #:_____
Notes:_____
_____

Name:_____
URL:_____
Login:_____
P/W:_____
Pin:_____
Security Questions:_____
_____
Account #:_____
Notes:_____
_____

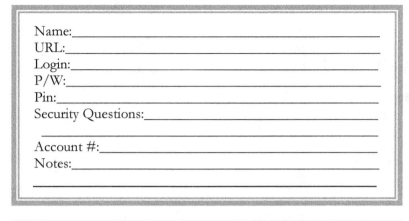

Name:_____
URL:_____
Login:_____
P/W:_____
Pin:_____
Security Questions:_____
_____
Account #:_____
Notes:_____
_____

Name:_____
URL:_____
Login:_____
P/W:_____
Pin:_____
Security Questions:_____
_____
Account #:_____
Notes:_____
_____

Name:_____
URL:_____
Login:_____
P/W:_____
Pin:_____
Security Questions:_____
_____
Account #:_____
Notes:_____
_____

Name:_____
URL:_____
Login:_____
P/W:_____
Pin:_____
Security Questions:_____
_____
Account #:_____
Notes:_____
_____

Name:_____
URL:_____
Login:_____
P/W:_____
Pin:_____
Security Questions:_____
_____
Account #:_____
Notes:_____
_____

Name:_____
URL:_____
Login:_____
P/W:_____
Pin:_____
Security Questions:_____
_____
Account #:_____
Notes:_____
_____

Name:_____
URL:_____
Login:_____
P/W:_____
Pin:_____
Security Questions:_____
_____
Account #:_____
Notes:_____
_____

Name:_____
URL:_____
Login:_____
P/W:_____
Pin:_____
Security Questions:_____
_____
Account #:_____
Notes:_____
_____

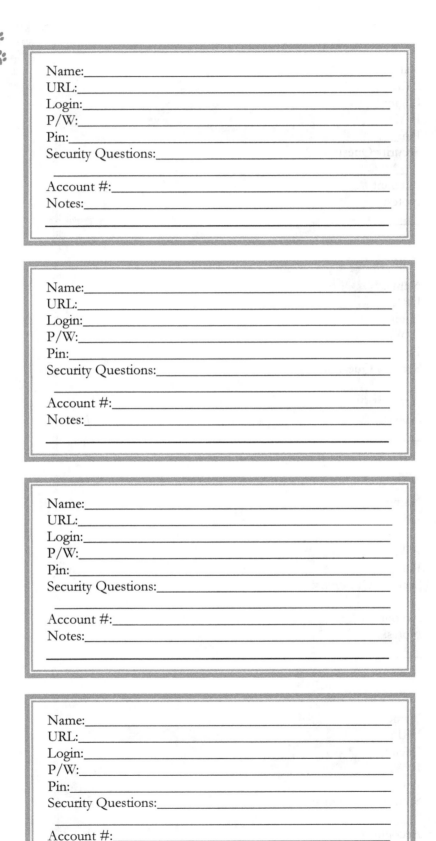

Name:_____

URL:_____

Login:_____

P/W:_____

Pin:_____

Security Questions:_____

_____

Account #:_____

Notes:_____

_____

Name:_____

URL:_____

Login:_____

P/W:_____

Pin:_____

Security Questions:_____

_____

Account #:_____

Notes:_____

_____

Name:_____

URL:_____

Login:_____

P/W:_____

Pin:_____

Security Questions:_____

_____

Account #:_____

Notes:_____

_____

Name:_____

URL:_____

Login:_____

P/W:_____

Pin:_____

Security Questions:_____

_____

Account #:_____

Notes:_____

_____

Name:_____
URL:_____
Login:_____
P/W:_____
Pin:_____
Security Questions:_____
_____
Account #:_____
Notes:_____
_____

Name:_____
URL:_____
Login:_____
P/W:_____
Pin:_____
Security Questions:_____
_____
Account #:_____
Notes:_____
_____

Name:_____
URL:_____
Login:_____
P/W:_____
Pin:_____
Security Questions:_____
_____
Account #:_____
Notes:_____
_____

Name:_____
URL:_____
Login:_____
P/W:_____
Pin:_____
Security Questions:_____
_____
Account #:_____
Notes:_____
_____

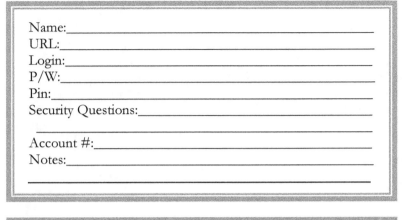

Name:_____
URL:_____
Login:_____
P/W:_____
Pin:_____
Security Questions:_____
_____
Account #:_____
Notes:_____
_____

Name:_____
URL:_____
Login:_____
P/W:_____
Pin:_____
Security Questions:_____
_____
Account #:_____
Notes:_____
_____

Name:_____
URL:_____
Login:_____
P/W:_____
Pin:_____
Security Questions:_____
_____
Account #:_____
Notes:_____
_____

Name:_____
URL:_____
Login:_____
P/W:_____
Pin:_____
Security Questions:_____
_____
Account #:_____
Notes:_____
_____

Name:_____
URL:_____
Login:_____
P/W:_____
Pin:_____
Security Questions:_____
_____
Account #:_____
Notes:_____
_____

Name:_____
URL:_____
Login:_____
P/W:_____
Pin:_____
Security Questions:_____
_____
Account #:_____
Notes:_____
_____

Name:_____
URL:_____
Login:_____
P/W:_____
Pin:_____
Security Questions:_____
_____
Account #:_____
Notes:_____
_____

Name:_____
URL:_____
Login:_____
P/W:_____
Pin:_____
Security Questions:_____
_____
Account #:_____
Notes:_____
_____

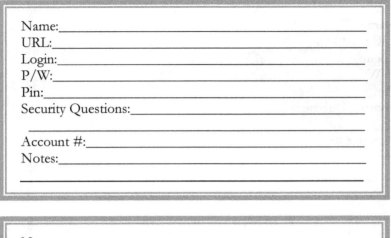

Name:_____
URL:_____
Login:_____
P/W:_____
Pin:_____
Security Questions:_____
_____
Account #:_____
Notes:_____
_____

Name:_____
URL:_____
Login:_____
P/W:_____
Pin:_____
Security Questions:_____
_____
Account #:_____
Notes:_____
_____

Name:_____
URL:_____
Login:_____
P/W:_____
Pin:_____
Security Questions:_____
_____
Account #:_____
Notes:_____
_____

Name:_____
URL:_____
Login:_____
P/W:_____
Pin:_____
Security Questions:_____
_____
Account #:_____
Notes:_____
_____

Name:_____
URL:_____
Login:_____
P/W:_____
Pin:_____
Security Questions:_____
_____
Account #:_____
Notes:_____
_____

Name:_____
URL:_____
Login:_____
P/W:_____
Pin:_____
Security Questions:_____
_____
Account #:_____
Notes:_____
_____

Name:_____
URL:_____
Login:_____
P/W:_____
Pin:_____
Security Questions:_____
_____
Account #:_____
Notes:_____
_____

Name:_____
URL:_____
Login:_____
P/W:_____
Pin:_____
Security Questions:_____
_____
Account #:_____
Notes:_____
_____

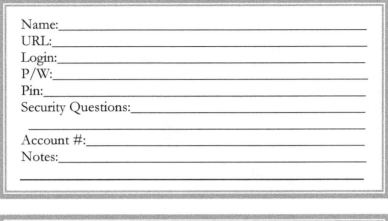

Name:_____

URL:_____

Login:_____

P/W:_____

Pin:_____

Security Questions:_____

_____

Account #:_____

Notes:_____

_____

Name:_____

URL:_____

Login:_____

P/W:_____

Pin:_____

Security Questions:_____

_____

Account #:_____

Notes:_____

_____

Name:_____

URL:_____

Login:_____

P/W:_____

Pin:_____

Security Questions:_____

_____

Account #:_____

Notes:_____

_____

Name:_____

URL:_____

Login:_____

P/W:_____

Pin:_____

Security Questions:_____

_____

Account #:_____

Notes:_____

_____

Name:_____
URL:_____
Login:_____
P/W:_____
Pin:_____
Security Questions:_____
_____
Account #:_____
Notes:_____
_____

Name:_____
URL:_____
Login:_____
P/W:_____
Pin:_____
Security Questions:_____
_____
Account #:_____
Notes:_____
_____

Name:_____
URL:_____
Login:_____
P/W:_____
Pin:_____
Security Questions:_____
_____
Account #:_____
Notes:_____
_____

Name:_____
URL:_____
Login:_____
P/W:_____
Pin:_____
Security Questions:_____
_____
Account #:_____
Notes:_____
_____

Name:_____
URL:_____
Login:_____
P/W:_____
Pin:_____
Security Questions:_____
_____
Account #:_____
Notes:_____
_____

Name:_____
URL:_____
Login:_____
P/W:_____
Pin:_____
Security Questions:_____
_____
Account #:_____
Notes:_____
_____

Name:_____
URL:_____
Login:_____
P/W:_____
Pin:_____
Security Questions:_____
_____
Account #:_____
Notes:_____
_____

Name:_____
URL:_____
Login:_____
P/W:_____
Pin:_____
Security Questions:_____
_____
Account #:_____
Notes:_____
_____

Name:_____
URL:_____
Login:_____
P/W:_____
Pin:_____
Security Questions:_____
_____
Account #:_____
Notes:_____
_____

Name:_____
URL:_____
Login:_____
P/W:_____
Pin:_____
Security Questions:_____
_____
Account #:_____
Notes:_____
_____

Name:_____
URL:_____
Login:_____
P/W:_____
Pin:_____
Security Questions:_____
_____
Account #:_____
Notes:_____
_____

Name:_____
URL:_____
Login:_____
P/W:_____
Pin:_____
Security Questions:_____
_____
Account #:_____
Notes:_____
_____

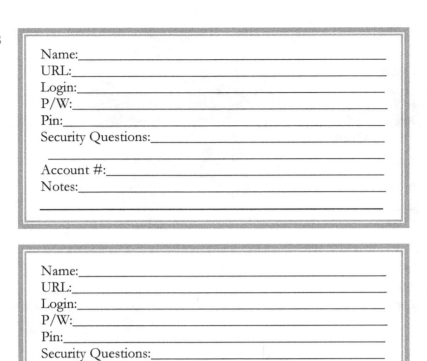

Name:_____
URL:_____
Login:_____
P/W:_____
Pin:_____
Security Questions:_____
_____
Account #:_____
Notes:_____
_____

Name:_____
URL:_____
Login:_____
P/W:_____
Pin:_____
Security Questions:_____
_____
Account #:_____
Notes:_____
_____

Name:_____
URL:_____
Login:_____
P/W:_____
Pin:_____
Security Questions:_____
_____
Account #:_____
Notes:_____
_____

Name:_____
URL:_____
Login:_____
P/W:_____
Pin:_____
Security Questions:_____
_____
Account #:_____
Notes:_____
_____

Ziggy's Secrets

Name:_____
URL:_____
Login:_____
P/W:_____
Pin:_____
Security Questions:_____
_____
Account #:_____
Notes:_____
_____

Name:_____
URL:_____
Login:_____
P/W:_____
Pin:_____
Security Questions:_____
_____
Account #:_____
Notes:_____
_____

Name:_____
URL:_____
Login:_____
P/W:_____
Pin:_____
Security Questions:_____
_____
Account #:_____
Notes:_____
_____

Name:_____
URL:_____
Login:_____
P/W:_____
Pin:_____
Security Questions:_____
_____
Account #:_____
Notes:_____
_____

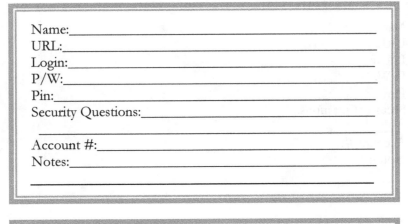

Name:_____

URL:_____

Login:_____

P/W:_____

Pin:_____

Security Questions:_____

_____

Account #:_____

Notes:_____

_____

Name:_____

URL:_____

Login:_____

P/W:_____

Pin:_____

Security Questions:_____

_____

Account #:_____

Notes:_____

_____

Name:_____

URL:_____

Login:_____

P/W:_____

Pin:_____

Security Questions:_____

_____

Account #:_____

Notes:_____

_____

Name:_____

URL:_____

Login:_____

P/W:_____

Pin:_____

Security Questions:_____

_____

Account #:_____

Notes:_____

_____

Name:_____
URL:_____
Login:_____
P/W:_____
Pin:_____
Security Questions:_____
_____
Account #:_____
Notes:_____
_____

Name:_____
URL:_____
Login:_____
P/W:_____
Pin:_____
Security Questions:_____
_____
Account #:_____
Notes:_____
_____

Name:_____
URL:_____
Login:_____
P/W:_____
Pin:_____
Security Questions:_____
_____
Account #:_____
Notes:_____
_____

Name:_____
URL:_____
Login:_____
P/W:_____
Pin:_____
Security Questions:_____
_____
Account #:_____
Notes:_____
_____

Name:_____
URL:_____
Login:_____
P/W:_____
Pin:_____
Security Questions:_____
_____
Account #:_____
Notes:_____
_____

Name:_____
URL:_____
Login:_____
P/W:_____
Pin:_____
Security Questions:_____
_____
Account #:_____
Notes:_____
_____

Name:_____
URL:_____
Login:_____
P/W:_____
Pin:_____
Security Questions:_____
_____
Account #:_____
Notes:_____
_____

Name:_____
URL:_____
Login:_____
P/W:_____
Pin:_____
Security Questions:_____
_____
Account #:_____
Notes:_____
_____

Name:_____
URL:_____
Login:_____
P/W:_____
Pin:_____
Security Questions:_____
_____
Account #:_____
Notes:_____
_____

Name:_____
URL:_____
Login:_____
P/W:_____
Pin:_____
Security Questions:_____
_____
Account #:_____
Notes:_____
_____

Name:_____
URL:_____
Login:_____
P/W:_____
Pin:_____
Security Questions:_____
_____
Account #:_____
Notes:_____
_____

Name:_____
URL:_____
Login:_____
P/W:_____
Pin:_____
Security Questions:_____
_____
Account #:_____
Notes:_____
_____

Name:_____
URL:_____
Login:_____
P/W:_____
Pin:_____
Security Questions:_____
_____
Account #:_____
Notes:_____
_____

Name:_____
URL:_____
Login:_____
P/W:_____
Pin:_____
Security Questions:_____
_____
Account #:_____
Notes:_____
_____

Name:_____
URL:_____
Login:_____
P/W:_____
Pin:_____
Security Questions:_____
_____
Account #:_____
Notes:_____
_____

Name:_____
URL:_____
Login:_____
P/W:_____
Pin:_____
Security Questions:_____
_____
Account #:_____
Notes:_____
_____

Name:_____
URL:_____
Login:_____
P/W:_____
Pin:_____
Security Questions:_____
_____
Account #:_____
Notes:_____
_____

Name:_____
URL:_____
Login:_____
P/W:_____
Pin:_____
Security Questions:_____
_____
Account #:_____
Notes:_____
_____

Name:_____
URL:_____
Login:_____
P/W:_____
Pin:_____
Security Questions:_____
_____
Account #:_____
Notes:_____
_____

Name:_____
URL:_____
Login:_____
P/W:_____
Pin:_____
Security Questions:_____
_____
Account #:_____
Notes:_____
_____

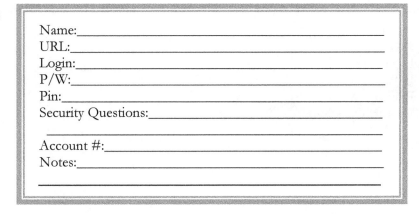

Name:_____

URL:_____

Login:_____

P/W:_____

Pin:_____

Security Questions:_____

_____

Account #:_____

Notes:_____

_____

Name:_____

URL:_____

Login:_____

P/W:_____

Pin:_____

Security Questions:_____

_____

Account #:_____

Notes:_____

_____

Name:_____

URL:_____

Login:_____

P/W:_____

Pin:_____

Security Questions:_____

_____

Account #:_____

Notes:_____

_____

Name:_____

URL:_____

Login:_____

P/W:_____

Pin:_____

Security Questions:_____

_____

Account #:_____

Notes:_____

_____

Name:_____
URL:_____
Login:_____
P/W:_____
Pin:_____
Security Questions:_____
_____
Account #:_____
Notes:_____
_____

Name:_____
URL:_____
Login:_____
P/W:_____
Pin:_____
Security Questions:_____
_____
Account #:_____
Notes:_____
_____

Name:_____
URL:_____
Login:_____
P/W:_____
Pin:_____
Security Questions:_____
_____
Account #:_____
Notes:_____
_____

Name:_____
URL:_____
Login:_____
P/W:_____
Pin:_____
Security Questions:_____
_____
Account #:_____
Notes:_____
_____

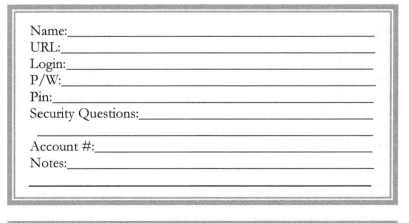

Name:_____

URL:_____

Login:_____

P/W:_____

Pin:_____

Security Questions:_____

_____

Account #:_____

Notes:_____

_____

Name:_____

URL:_____

Login:_____

P/W:_____

Pin:_____

Security Questions:_____

_____

Account #:_____

Notes:_____

_____

Name:_____

URL:_____

Login:_____

P/W:_____

Pin:_____

Security Questions:_____

_____

Account #:_____

Notes:_____

_____

Name:_____

URL:_____

Login:_____

P/W:_____

Pin:_____

Security Questions:_____

_____

Account #:_____

Notes:_____

_____

Name:_____
URL:_____
Login:_____
P/W:_____
Pin:_____
Security Questions:_____
_____
Account #:_____
Notes:_____
_____

Name:_____
URL:_____
Login:_____
P/W:_____
Pin:_____
Security Questions:_____
_____
Account #:_____
Notes:_____
_____

Name:_____
URL:_____
Login:_____
P/W:_____
Pin:_____
Security Questions:_____
_____
Account #:_____
Notes:_____
_____

Name:_____
URL:_____
Login:_____
P/W:_____
Pin:_____
Security Questions:_____
_____
Account #:_____
Notes:_____
_____

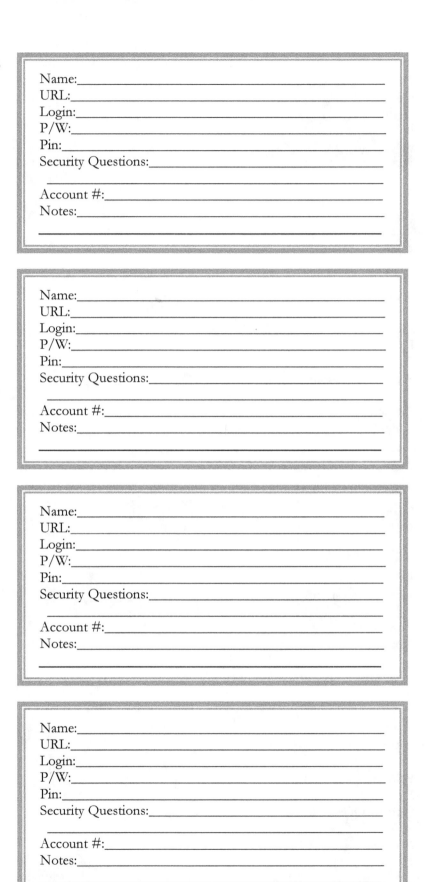

Name:_____

URL:_____

Login:_____

P/W:_____

Pin:_____

Security Questions:_____

_____

Account #:_____

Notes:_____

_____

Name:_____

URL:_____

Login:_____

P/W:_____

Pin:_____

Security Questions:_____

_____

Account #:_____

Notes:_____

_____

Name:_____

URL:_____

Login:_____

P/W:_____

Pin:_____

Security Questions:_____

_____

Account #:_____

Notes:_____

_____

Name:_____

URL:_____

Login:_____

P/W:_____

Pin:_____

Security Questions:_____

_____

Account #:_____

Notes:_____

_____

Name:_____
URL:_____
Login:_____
P/W:_____
Pin:_____
Security Questions:_____
_____
Account #:_____
Notes:_____
_____

Name:_____
URL:_____
Login:_____
P/W:_____
Pin:_____
Security Questions:_____
_____
Account #:_____
Notes:_____
_____

Name:_____
URL:_____
Login:_____
P/W:_____
Pin:_____
Security Questions:_____
_____
Account #:_____
Notes:_____
_____

Name:_____
URL:_____
Login:_____
P/W:_____
Pin:_____
Security Questions:_____
_____
Account #:_____
Notes:_____
_____

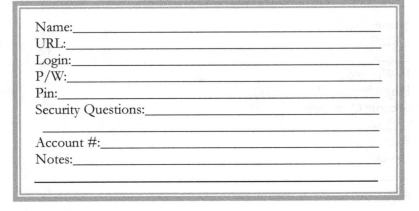

Name:_____
URL:_____
Login:_____
P/W:_____
Pin:_____
Security Questions:_____
_____
Account #:_____
Notes:_____
_____

Name:_____
URL:_____
Login:_____
P/W:_____
Pin:_____
Security Questions:_____
_____
Account #:_____
Notes:_____
_____

Name:_____
URL:_____
Login:_____
P/W:_____
Pin:_____
Security Questions:_____
_____
Account #:_____
Notes:_____
_____

Name:_____
URL:_____
Login:_____
P/W:_____
Pin:_____
Security Questions:_____
_____
Account #:_____
Notes:_____
_____

Name:_____
URL:_____
Login:_____
P/W:_____
Pin:_____
Security Questions:_____
_____
Account #:_____
Notes:_____
_____

Name:_____
URL:_____
Login:_____
P/W:_____
Pin:_____
Security Questions:_____
_____
Account #:_____
Notes:_____
_____

Name:_____
URL:_____
Login:_____
P/W:_____
Pin:_____
Security Questions:_____
_____
Account #:_____
Notes:_____
_____

Name:_____
URL:_____
Login:_____
P/W:_____
Pin:_____
Security Questions:_____
_____
Account #:_____
Notes:_____
_____

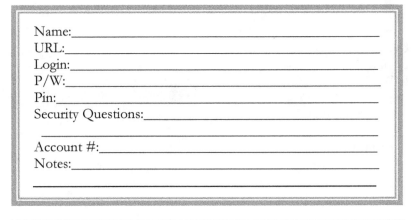

Name:_____

URL:_____

Login:_____

P/W:_____

Pin:_____

Security Questions:_____

_____

Account #:_____

Notes:_____

_____

Name:_____

URL:_____

Login:_____

P/W:_____

Pin:_____

Security Questions:_____

_____

Account #:_____

Notes:_____

_____

Name:_____

URL:_____

Login:_____

P/W:_____

Pin:_____

Security Questions:_____

_____

Account #:_____

Notes:_____

_____

Name:_____

URL:_____

Login:_____

P/W:_____

Pin:_____

Security Questions:_____

_____

Account #:_____

Notes:_____

_____

Name:_____
URL:_____
Login:_____
P/W:_____
Pin:_____
Security Questions:_____

_____
Account #:_____
Notes:_____

_____

Name:_____
URL:_____
Login:_____
P/W:_____
Pin:_____
Security Questions:_____

_____
Account #:_____
Notes:_____

_____

Name:_____
URL:_____
Login:_____
P/W:_____
Pin:_____
Security Questions:_____

_____
Account #:_____
Notes:_____

_____

Name:_____
URL:_____
Login:_____
P/W:_____
Pin:_____
Security Questions:_____

_____
Account #:_____
Notes:_____

_____

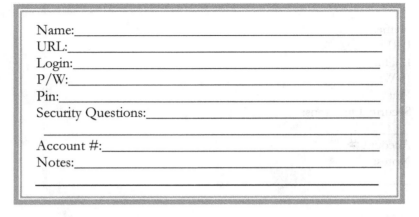

Name:_____
URL:_____
Login:_____
P/W:_____
Pin:_____
Security Questions:_____
_____
Account #:_____
Notes:_____
_____

Name:_____
URL:_____
Login:_____
P/W:_____
Pin:_____
Security Questions:_____
_____
Account #:_____
Notes:_____
_____

Name:_____
URL:_____
Login:_____
P/W:_____
Pin:_____
Security Questions:_____
_____
Account #:_____
Notes:_____
_____

Name:_____
URL:_____
Login:_____
P/W:_____
Pin:_____
Security Questions:_____
_____
Account #:_____
Notes:_____
_____

Name:_____
URL:_____
Login:_____
P/W:_____
Pin:_____
Security Questions:_____
_____
Account #:_____
Notes:_____
_____

Name:_____
URL:_____
Login:_____
P/W:_____
Pin:_____
Security Questions:_____
_____
Account #:_____
Notes:_____
_____

Name:_____
URL:_____
Login:_____
P/W:_____
Pin:_____
Security Questions:_____
_____
Account #:_____
Notes:_____
_____

Name:_____
URL:_____
Login:_____
P/W:_____
Pin:_____
Security Questions:_____
_____
Account #:_____
Notes:_____
_____

Name:_____
URL:_____
Login:_____
P/W:_____
Pin:_____
Security Questions:_____
_____
Account #:_____
Notes:_____
_____

Name:_____
URL:_____
Login:_____
P/W:_____
Pin:_____
Security Questions:_____
_____
Account #:_____
Notes:_____
_____

Name:_____
URL:_____
Login:_____
P/W:_____
Pin:_____
Security Questions:_____
_____
Account #:_____
Notes:_____
_____

Name:_____
URL:_____
Login:_____
P/W:_____
Pin:_____
Security Questions:_____
_____
Account #:_____
Notes:_____
_____

Name:_____
URL:_____
Login:_____
P/W:_____
Pin:_____
Security Questions:_____
_____
Account #:_____
Notes:_____
_____

Name:_____
URL:_____
Login:_____
P/W:_____
Pin:_____
Security Questions:_____
_____
Account #:_____
Notes:_____
_____

Name:_____
URL:_____
Login:_____
P/W:_____
Pin:_____
Security Questions:_____
_____
Account #:_____
Notes:_____
_____

Name:_____
URL:_____
Login:_____
P/W:_____
Pin:_____
Security Questions:_____
_____
Account #:_____
Notes:_____
_____

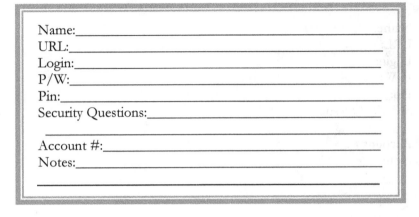

Name:_____

URL:_____

Login:_____

P/W:_____

Pin:_____

Security Questions:_____

_____

Account #:_____

Notes:_____

_____

Name:_____

URL:_____

Login:_____

P/W:_____

Pin:_____

Security Questions:_____

_____

Account #:_____

Notes:_____

_____

Name:_____

URL:_____

Login:_____

P/W:_____

Pin:_____

Security Questions:_____

_____

Account #:_____

Notes:_____

_____

Name:_____

URL:_____

Login:_____

P/W:_____

Pin:_____

Security Questions:_____

_____

Account #:_____

Notes:_____

_____

Name:_____
URL:_____
Login:_____
P/W:_____
Pin:_____
Security Questions:_____
_____
Account #:_____
Notes:_____
_____

Name:_____
URL:_____
Login:_____
P/W:_____
Pin:_____
Security Questions:_____
_____
Account #:_____
Notes:_____
_____

Name:_____
URL:_____
Login:_____
P/W:_____
Pin:_____
Security Questions:_____
_____
Account #:_____
Notes:_____
_____

Name:_____
URL:_____
Login:_____
P/W:_____
Pin:_____
Security Questions:_____
_____
Account #:_____
Notes:_____
_____

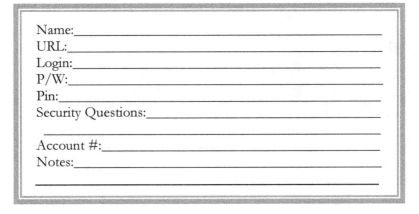

Name:_____

URL:_____

Login:_____

P/W:_____

Pin:_____

Security Questions:_____

_____

Account #:_____

Notes:_____

_____

Name:_____

URL:_____

Login:_____

P/W:_____

Pin:_____

Security Questions:_____

_____

Account #:_____

Notes:_____

_____

Name:_____

URL:_____

Login:_____

P/W:_____

Pin:_____

Security Questions:_____

_____

Account #:_____

Notes:_____

_____

Name:_____

URL:_____

Login:_____

P/W:_____

Pin:_____

Security Questions:_____

_____

Account #:_____

Notes:_____

_____

Name:_____
URL:_____
Login:_____
P/W:_____
Pin:_____
Security Questions:_____
_____
Account #:_____
Notes:_____
_____

Name:_____
URL:_____
Login:_____
P/W:_____
Pin:_____
Security Questions:_____
_____
Account #:_____
Notes:_____
_____

Name:_____
URL:_____
Login:_____
P/W:_____
Pin:_____
Security Questions:_____
_____
Account #:_____
Notes:_____
_____

Name:_____
URL:_____
Login:_____
P/W:_____
Pin:_____
Security Questions:_____
_____
Account #:_____
Notes:_____
_____

Name:_____
URL:_____
Login:_____
P/W:_____
Pin:_____
Security Questions:_____
_____
Account #:_____
Notes:_____
_____

Name:_____
URL:_____
Login:_____
P/W:_____
Pin:_____
Security Questions:_____
_____
Account #:_____
Notes:_____
_____

Name:_____
URL:_____
Login:_____
P/W:_____
Pin:_____
Security Questions:_____
_____
Account #:_____
Notes:_____
_____

Name:_____
URL:_____
Login:_____
P/W:_____
Pin:_____
Security Questions:_____
_____
Account #:_____
Notes:_____
_____

Name:_____
URL:_____
Login:_____
P/W:_____
Pin:_____
Security Questions:_____
_____
Account #:_____
Notes:_____
_____

Name:_____
URL:_____
Login:_____
P/W:_____
Pin:_____
Security Questions:_____
_____
Account #:_____
Notes:_____
_____

Name:_____
URL:_____
Login:_____
P/W:_____
Pin:_____
Security Questions:_____
_____
Account #:_____
Notes:_____
_____

Name:_____
URL:_____
Login:_____
P/W:_____
Pin:_____
Security Questions:_____
_____
Account #:_____
Notes:_____
_____

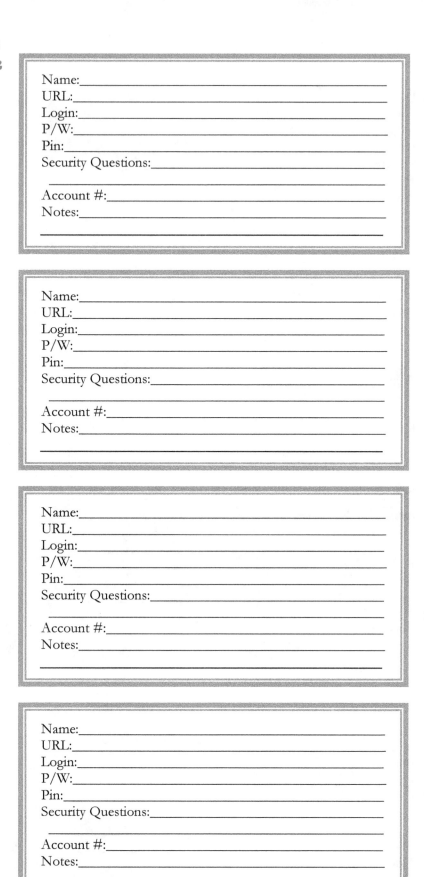

Name:_____

URL:_____

Login:_____

P/W:_____

Pin:_____

Security Questions:_____

_____

Account #:_____

Notes:_____

_____

Name:_____

URL:_____

Login:_____

P/W:_____

Pin:_____

Security Questions:_____

_____

Account #:_____

Notes:_____

_____

Name:_____

URL:_____

Login:_____

P/W:_____

Pin:_____

Security Questions:_____

_____

Account #:_____

Notes:_____

_____

Name:_____

URL:_____

Login:_____

P/W:_____

Pin:_____

Security Questions:_____

_____

Account #:_____

Notes:_____

_____

Name:_____
URL:_____
Login:_____
P/W:_____
Pin:_____
Security Questions:_____
_____
Account #:_____
Notes:_____
_____

Name:_____
URL:_____
Login:_____
P/W:_____
Pin:_____
Security Questions:_____
_____
Account #:_____
Notes:_____
_____

Name:_____
URL:_____
Login:_____
P/W:_____
Pin:_____
Security Questions:_____
_____
Account #:_____
Notes:_____
_____

Name:_____
URL:_____
Login:_____
P/W:_____
Pin:_____
Security Questions:_____
_____
Account #:_____
Notes:_____
_____

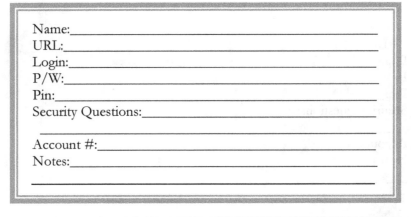

Name:_____

URL:_____

Login:_____

P/W:_____

Pin:_____

Security Questions:_____

_____

Account #:_____

Notes:_____

_____

Name:_____

URL:_____

Login:_____

P/W:_____

Pin:_____

Security Questions:_____

_____

Account #:_____

Notes:_____

_____

Name:_____

URL:_____

Login:_____

P/W:_____

Pin:_____

Security Questions:_____

_____

Account #:_____

Notes:_____

_____

Name:_____

URL:_____

Login:_____

P/W:_____

Pin:_____

Security Questions:_____

_____

Account #:_____

Notes:_____

_____

Name:_____
URL:_____
Login:_____
P/W:_____
Pin:_____
Security Questions:_____
_____
Account #:_____
Notes:_____
_____

Name:_____
URL:_____
Login:_____
P/W:_____
Pin:_____
Security Questions:_____
_____
Account #:_____
Notes:_____
_____

Name:_____
URL:_____
Login:_____
P/W:_____
Pin:_____
Security Questions:_____
_____
Account #:_____
Notes:_____
_____

Name:_____
URL:_____
Login:_____
P/W:_____
Pin:_____
Security Questions:_____
_____
Account #:_____
Notes:_____
_____

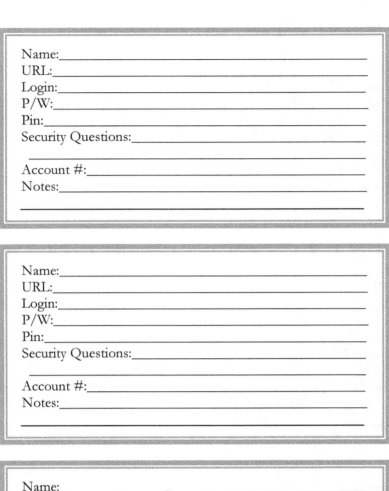

Name:_____
URL:_____
Login:_____
P/W:_____
Pin:_____
Security Questions:_____
_____
Account #:_____
Notes:_____
_____

Name:_____
URL:_____
Login:_____
P/W:_____
Pin:_____
Security Questions:_____
_____
Account #:_____
Notes:_____
_____

Name:_____
URL:_____
Login:_____
P/W:_____
Pin:_____
Security Questions:_____
_____
Account #:_____
Notes:_____
_____

Name:_____
URL:_____
Login:_____
P/W:_____
Pin:_____
Security Questions:_____
_____
Account #:_____
Notes:_____
_____

Name:_____
URL:_____
Login:_____
P/W:_____
Pin:_____
Security Questions:_____
_____
Account #:_____
Notes:_____
_____

Name:_____
URL:_____
Login:_____
P/W:_____
Pin:_____
Security Questions:_____
_____
Account #:_____
Notes:_____
_____

Name:_____
URL:_____
Login:_____
P/W:_____
Pin:_____
Security Questions:_____
_____
Account #:_____
Notes:_____
_____

Name:_____
URL:_____
Login:_____
P/W:_____
Pin:_____
Security Questions:_____
_____
Account #:_____
Notes:_____
_____

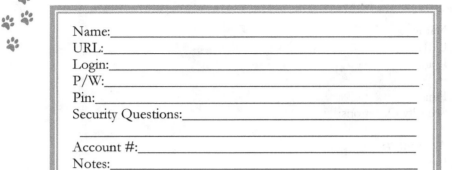

Name:_____

URL:_____

Login:_____

P/W:_____

Pin:_____

Security Questions:_____

_____

Account #:_____

Notes:_____

_____

Name:_____

URL:_____

Login:_____

P/W:_____

Pin:_____

Security Questions:_____

_____

Account #:_____

Notes:_____

_____

Name:_____

URL:_____

Login:_____

P/W:_____

Pin:_____

Security Questions:_____

_____

Account #:_____

Notes:_____

_____

Name:_____

URL:_____

Login:_____

P/W:_____

Pin:_____

Security Questions:_____

_____

Account #:_____

Notes:_____

_____

Name:_____
URL:_____
Login:_____
P/W:_____
Pin:_____
Security Questions:_____
_____
Account #:_____
Notes:_____
_____

Name:_____
URL:_____
Login:_____
P/W:_____
Pin:_____
Security Questions:_____
_____
Account #:_____
Notes:_____
_____

Name:_____
URL:_____
Login:_____
P/W:_____
Pin:_____
Security Questions:_____
_____
Account #:_____
Notes:_____
_____

Name:_____
URL:_____
Login:_____
P/W:_____
Pin:_____
Security Questions:_____
_____
Account #:_____
Notes:_____
_____

Name:_____
URL:_____
Login:_____
P/W:_____
Pin:_____
Security Questions:_____
_____
Account #:_____
Notes:_____
_____

Name:_____
URL:_____
Login:_____
P/W:_____
Pin:_____
Security Questions:_____
_____
Account #:_____
Notes:_____
_____

Name:_____
URL:_____
Login:_____
P/W:_____
Pin:_____
Security Questions:_____
_____
Account #:_____
Notes:_____
_____

Name:_____
URL:_____
Login:_____
P/W:_____
Pin:_____
Security Questions:_____
_____
Account #:_____
Notes:_____
_____

Name:_____
URL:_____
Login:_____
P/W:_____
Pin:_____
Security Questions:_____
_____
Account #:_____
Notes:_____
_____

Name:_____
URL:_____
Login:_____
P/W:_____
Pin:_____
Security Questions:_____
_____
Account #:_____
Notes:_____
_____

Name:_____
URL:_____
Login:_____
P/W:_____
Pin:_____
Security Questions:_____
_____
Account #:_____
Notes:_____
_____

Name:_____
URL:_____
Login:_____
P/W:_____
Pin:_____
Security Questions:_____
_____
Account #:_____
Notes:_____
_____

Name:_____
URL:_____
Login:_____
P/W:_____
Pin:_____
Security Questions:_____
_____
Account #:_____
Notes:_____
_____

Name:_____
URL:_____
Login:_____
P/W:_____
Pin:_____
Security Questions:_____
_____
Account #:_____
Notes:_____
_____

Name:_____
URL:_____
Login:_____
P/W:_____
Pin:_____
Security Questions:_____
_____
Account #:_____
Notes:_____
_____

Name:_____
URL:_____
Login:_____
P/W:_____
Pin:_____
Security Questions:_____
_____
Account #:_____
Notes:_____
_____

Name:_____
URL:_____
Login:_____
P/W:_____
Pin:_____
Security Questions:_____
_____
Account #:_____
Notes:_____
_____

Name:_____
URL:_____
Login:_____
P/W:_____
Pin:_____
Security Questions:_____
_____
Account #:_____
Notes:_____
_____

Name:_____
URL:_____
Login:_____
P/W:_____
Pin:_____
Security Questions:_____
_____
Account #:_____
Notes:_____
_____

Name:_____
URL:_____
Login:_____
P/W:_____
Pin:_____
Security Questions:_____
_____
Account #:_____
Notes:_____
_____

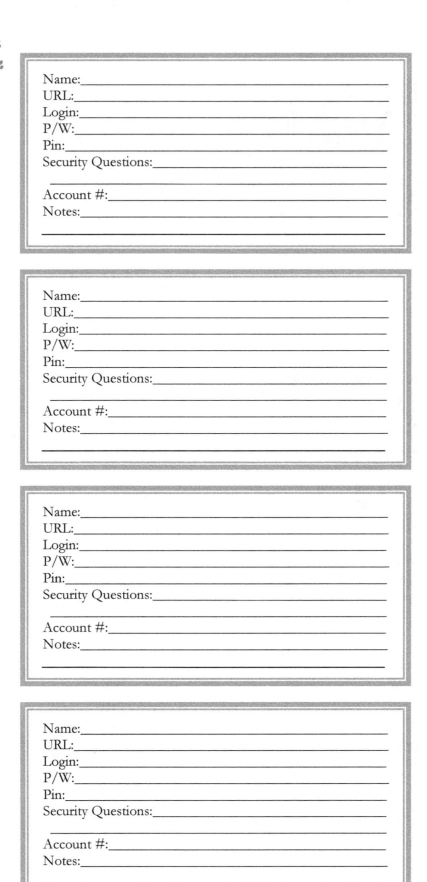

Name:_____

URL:_____

Login:_____

P/W:_____

Pin:_____

Security Questions:_____

_____

Account #:_____

Notes:_____

_____

Name:_____

URL:_____

Login:_____

P/W:_____

Pin:_____

Security Questions:_____

_____

Account #:_____

Notes:_____

_____

Name:_____

URL:_____

Login:_____

P/W:_____

Pin:_____

Security Questions:_____

_____

Account #:_____

Notes:_____

_____

Name:_____

URL:_____

Login:_____

P/W:_____

Pin:_____

Security Questions:_____

_____

Account #:_____

Notes:_____

_____

Name:_____
URL:_____
Login:_____
P/W:_____
Pin:_____
Security Questions:_____
_____
Account #:_____
Notes:_____
_____

Name:_____
URL:_____
Login:_____
P/W:_____
Pin:_____
Security Questions:_____
_____
Account #:_____
Notes:_____
_____

Name:_____
URL:_____
Login:_____
P/W:_____
Pin:_____
Security Questions:_____
_____
Account #:_____
Notes:_____
_____

Name:_____
URL:_____
Login:_____
P/W:_____
Pin:_____
Security Questions:_____
_____
Account #:_____
Notes:_____
_____

Name:_____
URL:_____
Login:_____
P/W:_____
Pin:_____
Security Questions:_____
_____
Account #:_____
Notes:_____
_____

Name:_____
URL:_____
Login:_____
P/W:_____
Pin:_____
Security Questions:_____
_____
Account #:_____
Notes:_____
_____

Name:_____
URL:_____
Login:_____
P/W:_____
Pin:_____
Security Questions:_____
_____
Account #:_____
Notes:_____
_____

Name:_____
URL:_____
Login:_____
P/W:_____
Pin:_____
Security Questions:_____
_____
Account #:_____
Notes:_____
_____

Name:_____
URL:_____
Login:_____
P/W:_____
Pin:_____
Security Questions:_____
_____
Account #:_____
Notes:_____
_____

Name:_____
URL:_____
Login:_____
P/W:_____
Pin:_____
Security Questions:_____
_____
Account #:_____
Notes:_____
_____

Name:_____
URL:_____
Login:_____
P/W:_____
Pin:_____
Security Questions:_____
_____
Account #:_____
Notes:_____
_____

Name:_____
URL:_____
Login:_____
P/W:_____
Pin:_____
Security Questions:_____
_____
Account #:_____
Notes:_____
_____

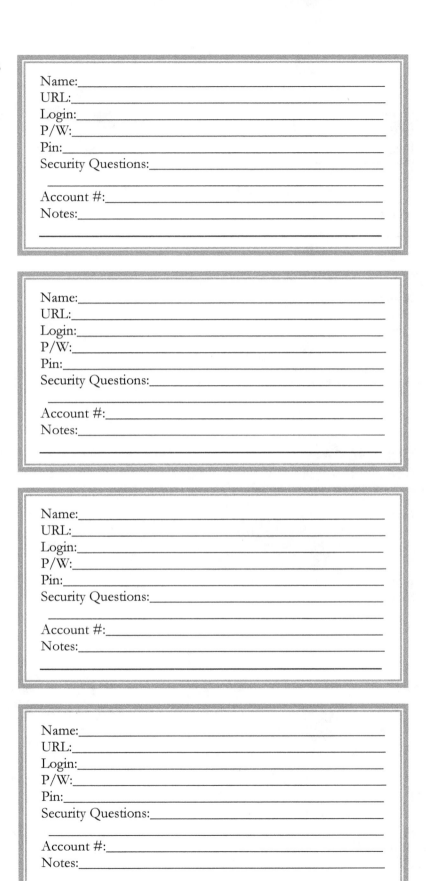

Name:_____

URL:_____

Login:_____

P/W:_____

Pin:_____

Security Questions:_____

_____

Account #:_____

Notes:_____

_____

Name:_____

URL:_____

Login:_____

P/W:_____

Pin:_____

Security Questions:_____

_____

Account #:_____

Notes:_____

_____

Name:_____

URL:_____

Login:_____

P/W:_____

Pin:_____

Security Questions:_____

_____

Account #:_____

Notes:_____

_____

Name:_____

URL:_____

Login:_____

P/W:_____

Pin:_____

Security Questions:_____

_____

Account #:_____

Notes:_____

_____

Name:_____
URL:_____
Login:_____
P/W:_____
Pin:_____
Security Questions:_____
_____
Account #:_____
Notes:_____
_____

Name:_____
URL:_____
Login:_____
P/W:_____
Pin:_____
Security Questions:_____
_____
Account #:_____
Notes:_____
_____

Name:_____
URL:_____
Login:_____
P/W:_____
Pin:_____
Security Questions:_____
_____
Account #:_____
Notes:_____
_____

Name:_____
URL:_____
Login:_____
P/W:_____
Pin:_____
Security Questions:_____
_____
Account #:_____
Notes:_____
_____

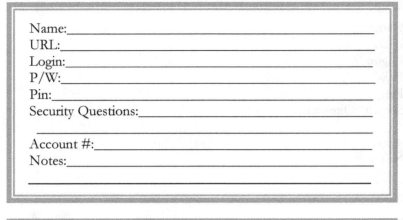

Name:_____
URL:_____
Login:_____
P/W:_____
Pin:_____
Security Questions:_____
_____
Account #:_____
Notes:_____
_____

Name:_____
URL:_____
Login:_____
P/W:_____
Pin:_____
Security Questions:_____
_____
Account #:_____
Notes:_____
_____

Name:_____
URL:_____
Login:_____
P/W:_____
Pin:_____
Security Questions:_____
_____
Account #:_____
Notes:_____
_____

Name:_____
URL:_____
Login:_____
P/W:_____
Pin:_____
Security Questions:_____
_____
Account #:_____
Notes:_____
_____

Name:_____
URL:_____
Login:_____
P/W:_____
Pin:_____
Security Questions:_____
_____
Account #:_____
Notes:_____
_____

Name:_____
URL:_____
Login:_____
P/W:_____
Pin:_____
Security Questions:_____
_____
Account #:_____
Notes:_____
_____

Name:_____
URL:_____
Login:_____
P/W:_____
Pin:_____
Security Questions:_____
_____
Account #:_____
Notes:_____
_____

Name:_____
URL:_____
Login:_____
P/W:_____
Pin:_____
Security Questions:_____
_____
Account #:_____
Notes:_____
_____

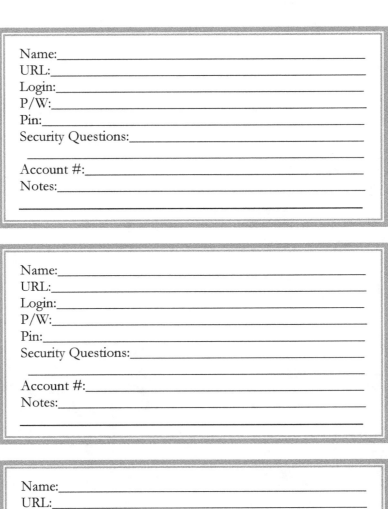

Name:_____

URL:_____

Login:_____

P/W:_____

Pin:_____

Security Questions:_____

_____

Account #:_____

Notes:_____

_____

Name:_____

URL:_____

Login:_____

P/W:_____

Pin:_____

Security Questions:_____

_____

Account #:_____

Notes:_____

_____

Name:_____

URL:_____

Login:_____

P/W:_____

Pin:_____

Security Questions:_____

_____

Account #:_____

Notes:_____

_____

Name:_____

URL:_____

Login:_____

P/W:_____

Pin:_____

Security Questions:_____

_____

Account #:_____

Notes:_____

_____

Name:_____
URL:_____
Login:_____
P/W:_____
Pin:_____
Security Questions:_____
_____
Account #:_____
Notes:_____
_____

Name:_____
URL:_____
Login:_____
P/W:_____
Pin:_____
Security Questions:_____
_____
Account #:_____
Notes:_____
_____

Name:_____
URL:_____
Login:_____
P/W:_____
Pin:_____
Security Questions:_____
_____
Account #:_____
Notes:_____
_____

Name:_____
URL:_____
Login:_____
P/W:_____
Pin:_____
Security Questions:_____
_____
Account #:_____
Notes:_____
_____

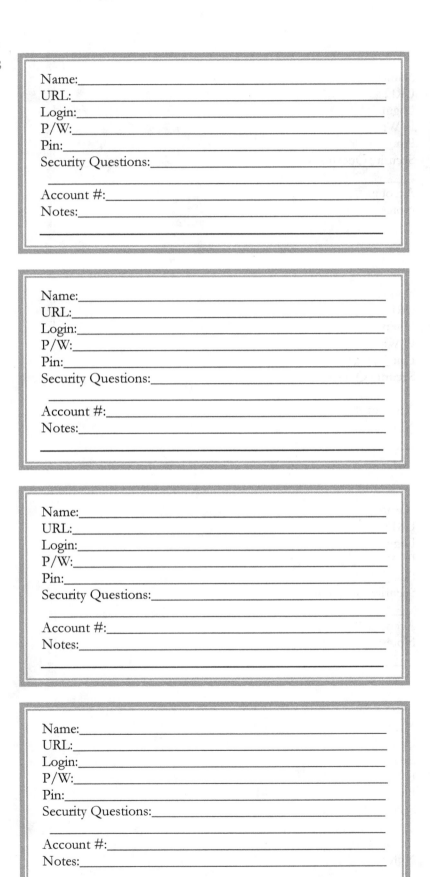

Name:_____

URL:_____

Login:_____

P/W:_____

Pin:_____

Security Questions:_____

_____

Account #:_____

Notes:_____

_____

Name:_____

URL:_____

Login:_____

P/W:_____

Pin:_____

Security Questions:_____

_____

Account #:_____

Notes:_____

_____

Name:_____

URL:_____

Login:_____

P/W:_____

Pin:_____

Security Questions:_____

_____

Account #:_____

Notes:_____

_____

Name:_____

URL:_____

Login:_____

P/W:_____

Pin:_____

Security Questions:_____

_____

Account #:_____

Notes:_____

_____

Name:_____
URL:_____
Login:_____
P/W:_____
Pin:_____
Security Questions:_____
_____
Account #:_____
Notes:_____
_____

Name:_____
URL:_____
Login:_____
P/W:_____
Pin:_____
Security Questions:_____
_____
Account #:_____
Notes:_____
_____

Name:_____
URL:_____
Login:_____
P/W:_____
Pin:_____
Security Questions:_____
_____
Account #:_____
Notes:_____
_____

Name:_____
URL:_____
Login:_____
P/W:_____
Pin:_____
Security Questions:_____
_____
Account #:_____
Notes:_____
_____

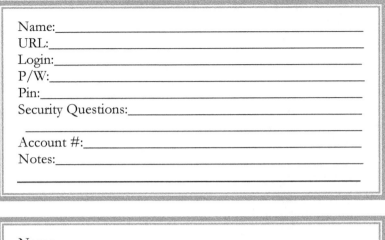

Name:_____
URL:_____
Login:_____
P/W:_____
Pin:_____
Security Questions:_____
_____
Account #:_____
Notes:_____
_____

Name:_____
URL:_____
Login:_____
P/W:_____
Pin:_____
Security Questions:_____
_____
Account #:_____
Notes:_____
_____

Name:_____
URL:_____
Login:_____
P/W:_____
Pin:_____
Security Questions:_____
_____
Account #:_____
Notes:_____
_____

Name:_____
URL:_____
Login:_____
P/W:_____
Pin:_____
Security Questions:_____
_____
Account #:_____
Notes:_____
_____

Name:_____
URL:_____
Login:_____
P/W:_____
Pin:_____
Security Questions:_____

_____
Account #:_____
Notes:_____

_____

Name:_____
URL:_____
Login:_____
P/W:_____
Pin:_____
Security Questions:_____

_____
Account #:_____
Notes:_____

_____

Name:_____
URL:_____
Login:_____
P/W:_____
Pin:_____
Security Questions:_____

_____
Account #:_____
Notes:_____

_____

Name:_____
URL:_____
Login:_____
P/W:_____
Pin:_____
Security Questions:_____

_____
Account #:_____
Notes:_____

_____

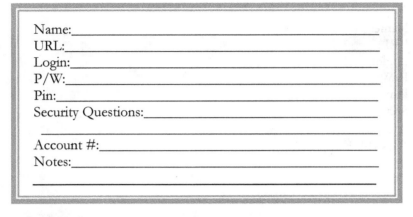

Name:_____

URL:_____

Login:_____

P/W:_____

Pin:_____

Security Questions:_____

_____

Account #:_____

Notes:_____

_____

Name:_____

URL:_____

Login:_____

P/W:_____

Pin:_____

Security Questions:_____

_____

Account #:_____

Notes:_____

_____

Name:_____

URL:_____

Login:_____

P/W:_____

Pin:_____

Security Questions:_____

_____

Account #:_____

Notes:_____

_____

Name:_____

URL:_____

Login:_____

P/W:_____

Pin:_____

Security Questions:_____

_____

Account #:_____

Notes:_____

_____

Name:_____
URL:_____
Login:_____
P/W:_____
Pin:_____
Security Questions:_____
_____
Account #:_____
Notes:_____
_____

Name:_____
URL:_____
Login:_____
P/W:_____
Pin:_____
Security Questions:_____
_____
Account #:_____
Notes:_____
_____

Name:_____
URL:_____
Login:_____
P/W:_____
Pin:_____
Security Questions:_____
_____
Account #:_____
Notes:_____
_____

Name:_____
URL:_____
Login:_____
P/W:_____
Pin:_____
Security Questions:_____
_____
Account #:_____
Notes:_____
_____

Name:_____

URL:_____

Login:_____

P/W:_____

Pin:_____

Security Questions:_____

_____

Account #:_____

Notes:_____

_____

Name:_____

URL:_____

Login:_____

P/W:_____

Pin:_____

Security Questions:_____

_____

Account #:_____

Notes:_____

_____

Name:_____

URL:_____

Login:_____

P/W:_____

Pin:_____

Security Questions:_____

_____

Account #:_____

Notes:_____

_____

Name:_____

URL:_____

Login:_____

P/W:_____

Pin:_____

Security Questions:_____

_____

Account #:_____

Notes:_____

_____

Name:_____
URL:_____
Login:_____
P/W:_____
Pin:_____
Security Questions:_____
_____
Account #:_____
Notes:_____
_____

Name:_____
URL:_____
Login:_____
P/W:_____
Pin:_____
Security Questions:_____
_____
Account #:_____
Notes:_____
_____

Name:_____
URL:_____
Login:_____
P/W:_____
Pin:_____
Security Questions:_____
_____
Account #:_____
Notes:_____
_____

Name:_____
URL:_____
Login:_____
P/W:_____
Pin:_____
Security Questions:_____
_____
Account #:_____
Notes:_____
_____

Name:_____
URL:_____
Login:_____
P/W:_____
Pin:_____
Security Questions:_____
_____
Account #:_____
Notes:_____
_____

Name:_____
URL:_____
Login:_____
P/W:_____
Pin:_____
Security Questions:_____
_____
Account #:_____
Notes:_____
_____

Name:_____
URL:_____
Login:_____
P/W:_____
Pin:_____
Security Questions:_____
_____
Account #:_____
Notes:_____
_____

Name:_____
URL:_____
Login:_____
P/W:_____
Pin:_____
Security Questions:_____
_____
Account #:_____
Notes:_____
_____

Name:_____
URL:_____
Login:_____
P/W:_____
Pin:_____
Security Questions:_____
_____
Account #:_____
Notes:_____
_____

Name:_____
URL:_____
Login:_____
P/W:_____
Pin:_____
Security Questions:_____
_____
Account #:_____
Notes:_____
_____

Name:_____
URL:_____
Login:_____
P/W:_____
Pin:_____
Security Questions:_____
_____
Account #:_____
Notes:_____
_____

Name:_____
URL:_____
Login:_____
P/W:_____
Pin:_____
Security Questions:_____
_____
Account #:_____
Notes:_____
_____

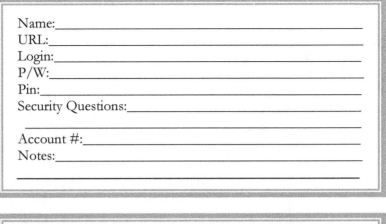

Name:_____

URL:_____

Login:_____

P/W:_____

Pin:_____

Security Questions:_____

_____

Account #:_____

Notes:_____

_____

Name:_____

URL:_____

Login:_____

P/W:_____

Pin:_____

Security Questions:_____

_____

Account #:_____

Notes:_____

_____

Name:_____

URL:_____

Login:_____

P/W:_____

Pin:_____

Security Questions:_____

_____

Account #:_____

Notes:_____

_____

Name:_____

URL:_____

Login:_____

P/W:_____

Pin:_____

Security Questions:_____

_____

Account #:_____

Notes:_____

_____

Name:_____
URL:_____
Login:_____
P/W:_____
Pin:_____
Security Questions:_____
_____
Account #:_____
Notes:_____
_____

Name:_____
URL:_____
Login:_____
P/W:_____
Pin:_____
Security Questions:_____
_____
Account #:_____
Notes:_____
_____

Name:_____
URL:_____
Login:_____
P/W:_____
Pin:_____
Security Questions:_____
_____
Account #:_____
Notes:_____
_____

Name:_____
URL:_____
Login:_____
P/W:_____
Pin:_____
Security Questions:_____
_____
Account #:_____
Notes:_____
_____

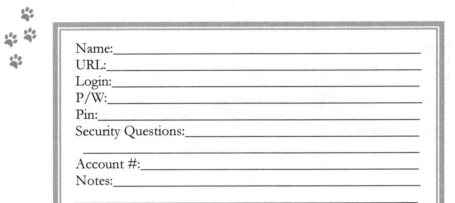

Name:_____
URL:_____
Login:_____
P/W:_____
Pin:_____
Security Questions:_____
_____
Account #:_____
Notes:_____
_____

Name:_____
URL:_____
Login:_____
P/W:_____
Pin:_____
Security Questions:_____
_____
Account #:_____
Notes:_____
_____

Name:_____
URL:_____
Login:_____
P/W:_____
Pin:_____
Security Questions:_____
_____
Account #:_____
Notes:_____
_____

Name:_____
URL:_____
Login:_____
P/W:_____
Pin:_____
Security Questions:_____
_____
Account #:_____
Notes:_____
_____

Name:_____
URL:_____
Login:_____
P/W:_____
Pin:_____
Security Questions:_____

_____
Account #:_____
Notes:_____

_____

Name:_____
URL:_____
Login:_____
P/W:_____
Pin:_____
Security Questions:_____

_____
Account #:_____
Notes:_____

_____

Name:_____
URL:_____
Login:_____
P/W:_____
Pin:_____
Security Questions:_____

_____
Account #:_____
Notes:_____

_____

Name:_____
URL:_____
Login:_____
P/W:_____
Pin:_____
Security Questions:_____

_____
Account #:_____
Notes:_____

_____

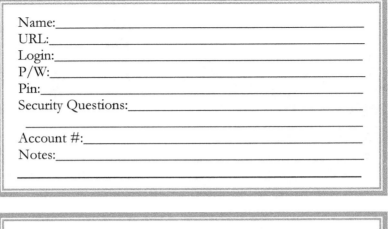

Name:_____
URL:_____
Login:_____
P/W:_____
Pin:_____
Security Questions:_____
_____
Account #:_____
Notes:_____
_____

Name:_____
URL:_____
Login:_____
P/W:_____
Pin:_____
Security Questions:_____
_____
Account #:_____
Notes:_____
_____

Name:_____
URL:_____
Login:_____
P/W:_____
Pin:_____
Security Questions:_____
_____
Account #:_____
Notes:_____
_____

Name:_____
URL:_____
Login:_____
P/W:_____
Pin:_____
Security Questions:_____
_____
Account #:_____
Notes:_____
_____

Additional Notes

Additional Notes

Additional Notes

Additional Notes

www.ingramcontent.com/pod-product-compliance
Lightning Source LLC
Chambersburg PA
CBHW060146060326
40690CB00018B/4008